Bergson
and the Stream of Consciousness Novel

Bergson
and the Stream of Consciousness Novel

Bergson

and the Stream of Consciousness Novel

BY SHIV K. KUMAR

Professor and Head of the Department of English, Osmania University, Hyderabad

"...*the steady monologuy of the interiors*...
their pardonable confusion...*by the light of*
philosophy...*things will begin to clear up a*
bit one way or another..."

FINNEGANS WAKE

New York University Press   *1963*

Library of Congress Catalog Card Number: 63-14035
©1962 by Shiv K. Kumar
Manufactured in the United States of America
First published in Great Britain by Blackie & Son Limited

Preface

THE KIND OF FICTION WHICH HAS COME TO BE
known as the stream of consciousness novel has aroused much controversy since the publication of Dorothy Richardson's *Pointed Roofs*
in 1915. Although many critics have analysed its various aspects,
none has, so far as I know, attempted to present a comprehensive
interpretation of its nature and scope in terms of Bergson's concept
of durational flux, which seems to provide an important clue to the
real creative impulse behind the new mode of portraying character
as a ceaseless stream of becoming. In other words, the basic issues
involved in this form of fiction are essentially of a metaphysical
nature, as is suggested by the preoccupation of various protagonists
in the novels of Dorothy Richardson, Virginia Woolf and James
Joyce with the ultimate nature of reality.

Of this new concept of experience as a process of qualitative
interpenetration of states of consciousness, Bergson's philosophy
seems to be the most comprehensive formulation; hence, "his
representative importance" (to quote André Gide). The late Miss
Dorothy Richardson corroborates the same view in a letter to this
author. "No doubt", she writes, "Bergson influenced many minds,
if only by putting into words something then dawning within the
human consciousness: an increased sense of the inadequacy of the
clock as a time-measurer".

My main purpose is, therefore, not to establish Bergson's direct influence on the novelists whom I discuss; I am rather concerned to bring out the *parallelism* between the notion of the stream of consciousness as it appears in these novelists and the Bergsonian concept of flux. It is possible that in Bergson's literary presentation of his philosophical theories, many a contemporary writer might have experienced a kind of self-realization. His poetic style, his suggestive similes and his vast store of literary reading, on which he invariably draws for suitable comparisons and analogies, make him the most 'literary' of all contemporary philosophers.

There are some studies of Bergsonism in contemporary literary criticism: for instance, Turquet-Milnes' *Some Modern French Writers (A Study in Bergsonism)*, Floris Delattre's *Les Études Bergsoniennes, Le Roman Psychologique de Virginia Woolf*, Thibaudet's *Le Bergsonisme,* and Wyndham Lewis's *Time and Western Man*. But Turquet-Milnes is exclusively concerned with modern French writers and Floris Delattre's Bergsonian analysis of Virginia Woolf is both incomplete and inadequate; while Wyndham Lewis fails to render an impartial "analysis of the mind of James Joyce" (a chapter in *Time and Western Man*), violently prejudiced as he is against Bergsonism. Thibaudet's exposition of the new philosophy, although more comprehensive in scope than many other similar studies, does not fully explore the possibilities of its relation to the new trends in modern art and literature. Other studies like Hans Meyerhoff's *Time in Literature*, Mendilow's *Time and the Novel*, Georges Poulet's *Studies in Human Time*, Robert Humphrey's *Stream of Consciousness in the Modern Novel* Melvin Friedman's *Stream of Consciousness—a Study in Literary Method* etc., though commendable in many respects, have not inquired into the time-problem essentially from the Bergsonian point of view.

I have, therefore, ventured to explore in detail the various potentialities of a Bergsonian interpretation of the stream of consciousness novel to establish that Bergsonism alone offers a plausible and integrated explanation of the enigma of *le roman fleuve*.

The nature of this inquiry—a study of the stream of consciousness novel in terms of Bergsonian *durée*, intuition, *l'émotion créatrice, le langage dynamique,* etc.—obviously implies certain inevitable repetitions, and I have, at places, felt it necessary to provide long citations from the text mainly with a view to establishing as explicitly as possible the close parallelism between Bergsonism and the new technique.

Parts of this book have already appeared in *Modern Philology, The Journal of Aesthetics & Art Criticism, Notes & Queries, The Modern Language Review, The Canadian Modern Language Review, Modern Language Notes, Modern Language Quarterly, English Studies, The University of South Kansas City Review, Modern Fiction Studies, The Indian Journal of English Studies, The Literary Criterion, Osmania Journal of English Studies;* I wish to acknowledge courtesy of the editors and publishers of these journals for permission to reprint these materials.

I am grateful to Mr. T. S. Eliot, Mr. Clive Bell, Mr. Edmund Wilson for answering my queries and offering suggestions; I am particularly grateful to Mr. Stuart Gilbert for his constant help and encouragement, and for reading so carefully my chapter on "James Joyce"; to Mr. E. M. Forster and Mr. Leonard Woolf for reading the chapter on "Virginia Woolf". I am indebted to Professor W. Y. Tindall and Professor V. de S. Pinto for reading through the entire MS and for their generous appreciation. I am also thankful to the late Miss Dorothy Richardson who not only lent me some very useful material but also enlightened me on certain aspects of her work. To my wife, Anita S. Kumar, I am indebted for reading the proofs, offering useful comments—and for profounder reasons.

Finally I should express my deepest gratitude to Professor David Daiches for his invaluable suggestions, sympathetic criticism and encouragement. I owe him much more than I can render in words.

SHIV K. KUMAR

Osmania University,
Hyderabad-Deccan (India)

Acknowledgments

GRATEFUL ACKNOWLEDGMENTS ARE DUE TO THE following publishers and individuals for their kind permission to quote brief passages from copyright materials:

MESSRS. GEORGE ALLEN & UNWIN LTD. for the many quotations from the authorized translations of Bergson's *Matter and Memory* and *Time and Free Will*, both published by them, and readily obtainable;

MESSRS. JONATHAN CAPE LTD. for extracts from James Joyce's *A Portrait of the Artist as a Young Man* and *Stephen Hero*;

MESSRS. CHATTO & WINDUS LTD. for excerpts from *Letters of Proust* (translated by Nina Curtiss), *Time Regained* (translated by Stephen Hudson), *Swann's Way* (translated by S. Moncrieff), and *The Guermantes Way* (translated by S. Moncrieff);

MESSRS. J. M. DENT & SONS LTD. and ALFRED A. KNOPF INC. for extracts from the works of Dorothy Richardson;

MESSRS. MACMILLAN & CO. LTD. and MLLE. J. A. BERGSON for extracts from the works of Henri Bergson;

THE SOCIETY OF AUTHORS for extracts from the works of James Joyce;

MR. LEONARD WOOLF and MESSRS THE HOGARTH PRESS LTD. for passages from the works of Virginia Woolf.

To David Daiches

Contents

CHAPTER 1

Introduction

THE EMERGENCE OF THE STREAM OF CON-
sciousness novel in contemporary fiction has provoked much
controversy, but the basic issues involved still remain vague
and unexplained. The new form of narrative has been variously
defined, not infrequently from conflicting points of view; its
origins are traced to sources which fail to reveal the real
creative impulse behind this new mode of representing human
experience. All this confusion results from a fundamental
misunderstanding of the underlying intention of the new
novelist, who does not conceive character as a state but as a
process of ceaseless becoming in a medium which may be
termed Bergson's *durée réelle*.

Before inquiring into the full implications of this approach,
it may be useful here first to give a brief résumé of the various
theories which have so far been advanced to explain the nature
and scope of the new technique.

A popular theory, put forth by many critics, presents the
stream of consciousness method as an inevitable sequel to the
disintegration of values in the first quarter of this century,
and an attempt to compensate by excessive experimentation
for the spiritual vacuum prevailing everywhere. The new

novel, therefore, is a manifestation, says H. J. Muller, of "the blurring of objective reality and the dissolution of certainties in all fields of thought."[1] Professor Weidlé also seems to support this view when he attributes extreme cultivation of technique to the highly subjective modes of artistic apprehension, unrelated to any established code of values. Proust, Joyce, Svevo and others, in his opinion, embody in their work an exaggerated form of *principium individuationis*.[2] The new novel, therefore, is described as a withdrawal from external phenomena into the flickering half-shades of the author's private world. It will, however, be shown in the course of a detailed analysis of the work of Dorothy Richardson, Virginia Woolf and James Joyce that the new prose-fiction does not imply a "withdrawal" from objective reality but constitutes, on the contrary, a deliberate effort to render in a literary medium a new realization of experience as a process of dynamic renewal.

According to others, the new technique derives from the psycho-analytical school of Jung, Freud and Adler. The spirit of Zürich, it is suggested, broods over Joyce's Dublin, Virginia Woolf's and Dorothy Richardson's London. The "business of producing the psychological novel has much in common", says a critic, "with the business of being psychoanalysed",[3] and it is asserted that "the thought-stream novel usually can only be appreciated fully by people whose subconscious is in the same state as that of the author".[4] F. J. Hoffman and Pelham Edgar,[5] however, do not prescribe any such limits in their interpretation of the new technique. The former attempts to explain the purport of the stream of consciousness novelist as the representation of four different levels of consciousness:[6] the conscious, the preconscious, the subconscious and the unconscious, as if the author had undertaken to solve a complex psychological problem in terms of literary symbols.

Robert Humphrey stresses another psychological aspect

of the technique by defining it "as a type of fiction in which strong emphasis is placed on exploration of the pre-speech levels of consciousness for the purposes, primarily, of revealing the psychic being of the characters".[7] This type of fiction becomes for him "essentially a technical feat".[8]

Edward Bowling presents more or less the same view when he describes the new form of novel as "*a direct quotation of the mind*—not merely of the language area but of the whole consciousness".[9] The pre-speech area thus again forms a predominant part of the range covered by the stream of consciousness novelist, who attempts to externalize sensations and ideas not normally expressed by words and images. Professor J. W. Beach, on the other hand, emphasizes "exploitation of the element of incoherence in our conscious process" as the "defining feature" of the new technique.[10]

The interest of all stream of consciousness novelists in the contemporary psycho-analytical theories cannot be overestimated;[11] the danger lies only in exaggerating this relationship and reading their novels as mere "liberation of suppressions".[12] To label Dorothy Richardson's *Pilgrimage* as a document of "the Daphnean furtiveness of a woman's mind",[13] would be as inaccurate as to treat *Ulysses* as a text-book of psychology and psychiatry.[14] Nor again, would the work of Virginia Woolf yield any significant results if analysed in terms of psycho-analysis, since the stream of consciousness novelists are essentially concerned with presenting individual personality and experience in terms of artistic sensibility.

A psycho-analytical interpretation of the stream of consciousness novel would hardly illuminate its treatment and presentation of *la durée*, *mémoire involontaire* and intuition,[15] nor would it bring out the significance of the various protagonists' preoccupation with the ultimate nature of reality. It is here that Bergsonism attempts to reach out beyond the limits of psycho-analysis. In being more sympathetic towards aesthetic inclinations, more attuned to the mysterious nature of creative processes, Bergson's philosophical theories of time, memory and consciousness provide a more useful clue to the understanding of the new technique. The emergence of time as a new mode of artistic perception in the contemporary novel[16] would alone justify the Bergsonian approach as being more aesthetic than the mechanistic treatment of psychoanalysts.

The technique has also been described by some as a mere literary embellishment, a means of investing character, scene and incident with "wise bits of philosophy", or iridescent "flashes of beauty", lending to the entire narrative a touch of ethereality, of "something spirit-like".[17] This is how Ethel William Hawkins defines it—as something synonymous with a hypersensitive awareness of phenomena highly tinged with the observer's own evanescent moods. This theory obviously takes a very restricted view of the technique by ignoring altogether its aesthetic and philosophical implications.

This kind of novel has been analysed by others in terms of impressionistic painting, and referred to as "the Post-impressionistic Novel". "The problem of the twentieth-century novelist was the same as that of the twentieth-century painter".[18] Is the technique to be photographic or impressionistic? asks Professor Isaacs, and proceeds to show how even the phraseology and imagery in Virginia Woolf's famous essay "Modern Fiction" are full of echoes from such works as R. M. Stevenson's exposition of Velasquez's art.[19] These novelists, as Herbert Muller also affirms, have in various ways adapted to fiction the technique of the impressionistic painters, specially as it was supplemented by Cézanne.[20]

But a closer examination will show that beyond suggesting a certain similarity of aesthetic intention, this theory also fails to offer a satisfactory explanation of the new technique of characterization. It would be incorrect to say that Virginia Woolf, Dorothy Richardson or James Joyce was influenced by the impressionistic school of painting, which was itself a manifestation of the new awareness of reality as *"les données immédiates de la conscience"*.[21]

There is yet another school of criticism which relates the new technique to the symbolistic modes of expression. Speaking of the characters in *Ulysses,* Edmund Wilson remarks: "When we are admitted to the mind of any of them, we are in a world as complex and special, a world sometimes as fantastic or obscure, as that of the symbolist poet—and a world rendered by similar devices of language".[22] In his use of the interior monologue—"symbolistic monologues"—Joyce fully exploits, according to Edmund Wilson, "the methods of symbolism".[23] In their anti-mechanistic intentions, their emphasis on intimating things rather than stating them, their use of a complicated association of ideas, their insistence upon inventing a special language to express individual personality, the symbolists seem to imply a metaphysic similar to Bergsonism.[24] In fact, the work of James Joyce, Virginia Woolf and Dorothy Richardson is, in a certain sense, a continuation of symbolism.

But again, Bergsonism appears to offer a more comprehensive explanation of the literary and philosophical implications of the new novel than symbolism. Durational flux, which constitutes the essence of this technique, is obviously more Bergsonian than symbolistic in character, and the former in its wider scope seems to embrace the basic principles of the latter.

And lastly, the relation of the stream of consciousness narrative to such popular arts as the cinema has also been studied.[25] Harry Levin suggests a similarity between this technique and *montage* under which he analyses the various aspects of *le monologue intérieur.* "Bloom's mind", he observes, "is neither a *tabula rasa* nor a photographic plate, but a motion picture, which has been ingeniously cut and carefully edited to emphasize the close-ups and fade-outs of flickering emotion, the angles of observation and the flashbacks of reminiscence.

In its intimacy and in its continuity, *Ulysses* has more in common with the cinema than with other fiction. The movement of Joyce's style, the thought of his characters, is like unreeling film; his method of construction, the arrangement of this raw material, involves the crucial operation of *montage*."[26]

There may be some justification for each of these expositions[27] of the stream of consciousness novel, which has undoubtedly some elements in common with the post-impressionistic painting, the symbolist modes of expression, or even the cinema. But as mentioned earlier, none of these theories presents a comprehensive view and explains fully the precise nature and scope of the technique. The new novelist is neither exclusively an impressionistic delineator of character and scene, nor a psycho-analyst whose primary function is to render a clinical analysis of human motives and impulses.[28] Characters like Mrs. Dalloway, Miriam Henderson and Stephen Dedalus are self-sufficient, deriving their validity from their creator's vicarious experience. They do not require the help of a psycho-analyst for any fuller understanding of them, for the "business of producing the psychological novel" is *not* the same as "the business of being psycho-analysed". Nor again is the stream of consciousness technique an esoteric jigsaw of words and sentences,[29] implying a withdrawal from objective reality into the author's own private world.[30] On the contrary, this kind of novel seems to make a positive affirmation of a view of experience which can be apprehended better in terms of Bergson's durational flux.

Before investigating this parallelism more fully, it may be profitable to say a word about *le monologue intérieur* as employed by Edouard Dujardin, whose novel *Les Lauriers sont coupés* (1888) is supposed to have influenced James Joyce.[31] Dujardin is also responsible for popularizing in literary criticism this term which, according to him, was invented by Valery Larbaud; "L'invention de l'expression, dans le sens que nous lui donnons aujourd'hui, semble être dûe à Valery Larbaud lui-même."[32]

The credit, however, of originating the term *"monologue intérieur"* and presenting a detailed analysis of its various aspects, together with a comprehensive survey of its theory and practice in literary and philosophical history, belongs to Victor Egger who published in 1881 his scholarly treatise *La Parole Intérieure*. He defines it as "un des éléments les plus importants . . . de nos actes ; la série des mots intérieurs forme une succession presque continue . . . le moi et la durée sont des idées équivalentes . . . c'est le moi ; *je suis une pure succession*."[33]

Later in 1930 when Edouard Dujardin, in the course of a series of literary conferences, gave an elaborate analysis of the interior monologue, he had little to add to Victor Egger's definition of it. "Le monologue intérieur," says Dujardin, "est, dans l'ordre de la poésie, le discours sans auditeur et non prononcé . . ."[34]

The important point to note, however, is that both these commentators emphasize the element of fluidity in our states of consciousness. In the words of Dujardin: "la nouveauté *essentielle* qu'a apportée le monologue intérieur consiste en ce qu'il a pour objet d'évoquer *le flux ininterrompu* des pensées qui traversent l'âme du personnage . . ."[35]

It is precisely this inner *flux ininterrompu* that Bergson designates as *la durée*, a process of creative evolution which does not lend itself to any logical or intellectual analysis. *La durée* or psychological time thus becomes the distinguishing feature of the stream of consciousness novel. The new novelist accepts with full awareness inner duration against chronological time as the only true mode of apprehending aesthetic experience. Only in terms of the emergence of time as the fourth dimension can, therefore, one of the most important literary movements of this century be understood. "There is a plane geometry", writes Marcel Proust in a letter to his friend Antoine Bibesco, "and a geometry of space. And so for me the novel is not only plane psychology but psychology in space and time. *That invisible substance, time, I try to isolate.*"[36] Again, towards the end of *Remembrance of Things Past,* he sums up his entire aesthetic theory:

"I should endeavour to render that Time-dimension by transcribing life in a way very different from that conveyed by our lying senses . . . everybody feels that we are occupying an unceasingly increasing place in Time, and this universality could only rejoice me since it is the truth, a truth suspected by each one of us which it was my business to try to elucidate . . . If, at least, time enough were allotted to me to accomplish my work, I would not fail to mark it with the seal of Time . . . and I would therein describe men, if need be, as monsters occupying a place in Time infinitely more important than the restricted one reserved for them in space . . ."[37]

Every stream of consciousness novel bears this seal of time. Time, or as Bergson prefers to call it *la durée,* enters the field of creative thought as something incapable of measurement and intractable to such symbolical represent-ations as hours, days, months and years which are only its spatialized concepts. Edouard, André Gide's protagonist in *The Coiners,* enunciates his theory of the novel as a breadthwise and depthwise cutting of "a slice of life", in preference to "the naturalist school" that "always cuts its slice in the same direction; in time, lengthwise."[38] Gide, obviously, implies the durational as an integral mode of apprehension of reality as contrasted with the spatial rendering of life in fiction, for in the latter, time projected lengthwise is nothing but space.

The extent to which this new concept of time as an immeasurable and multidirectional process had permeated the European novel of the first quarter of this century, may be assessed from these novelists who employed this stream of consciousness method in representing *la durée.*

Jacques Goddard, Jules Romains's protagonist in *The*

Death of a Nobody, reflects on the theme of time; "In particular he had pondered upon time. Time seemed to him something quite arbitrary and elastic. He found it difficult to believe it was a dependable entity, and clocks seemed to him fallacious mechanisms for measuring it."[39]

A similar realization of the elasticity of time dawns within the consciousness of Italo Svevo's hero in *The Nice Old Man*:

"I, on the contrary, am obstinately trying to do something else in this present and if, as I hope, there is time to develop an activity in it, I shall have proved that it is longer than it appears. It is hard to measure it and the mathematician who tried to do so would come hopelessly to grief, thus showing that it is not his work."[40]

Virginia Woolf stresses this discrepancy between "time in the mind" and clock time more explicitly in *Orlando*.[41] Thomas Wolfe in *Look Homeward Angel*[42] and Gertrude Stein in *Composition as Explanation*,[43] affirm almost the same view of duration. The work of Dorothy Richardson and James Joyce is no less an illustration of this subjective notion of time.

This "time in the mind" is symbolically represented by most of these novelists as a flowing river with memories and visions as its chief constituents.[44] The flux of human experience consists in this perpetual mixing of memory with desire, making one "live in a mixed tense, as is man's lot, the grammar of which has, however, those pure tenses which seem made for the animals."[45] This "horrible activity of the mind's eye",[46] lies in our ceaseless response to a multiplicity of sensory impressions and recollections, the latter conditioning and therefore, in a sense, recreating each moment of experience. Time, no longer a mere extended image of space, now becomes the pure essence of reality, which may be described as "a succession of qualitative changes, which melt into and permeate one another, without precise outlines, without any tendency to externalize themselves in relation to one another";[47] or, as a principle "of becoming which is reality itself."[48]

The key to the emergence of the stream of consciousness novel lies in this new awareness of experience, this marked shift from a conception of personality as built round a hard and changeless core to a realization of it as a dynamic process. This reality is to be realized in immediate experience as flux, to be grasped by intuition or intellectual sympathy.[49] *La durée* is the stuff of which this kind of novel is made.

*   *   *   *   *   *

To understand completely the durational aspect of the new novel, it will be necessary to examine in detail the philosophical significance of the work of Marcel Proust,[50] who is often associated with certain aspects of the technique as employed by Dorothy Richardson, Virginia Woolf and James Joyce. It must, however, be admitted at the outset that Proust does not use the stream of consciousness method of narrative; in fact, instead of completely immersing himself in the stream of becoming, he retains the right to elucidate, analyse, comment and judge. But in most of his observations on the art of the novel, he seems to provide the new novelist with a suitable working credo.

Proust always claimed to have presented in his work "a whole theory of memory and consciousness, although not directly projected in logical terms."[51] In denouncing intellect as a spatializing tendency,[52] in recognizing the supremacy of involuntary memories over voluntary memories[53] and the validity of fugitive impressions as significant phenomena,[54] in endeavouring to bring reality within the fold of his work with the "least possible shrinkage", in "respecting" in the matter of style "the natural progress of my thought",[55] and lastly, in emphasizing the importance of *la durée* in a work of art, Proust supplies all the ingredients of the stream of consciousness technique, except, of course, its practical application.

The work of Proust has, therefore, a two-fold significance to the student of the stream of consciousness novel; first because many younger novelists found in him a confirmation of what was already dawning within their own minds, and secondly, because he proved to be, though quite unwittingly, a provocative introduction to Bergson's philosophy of time, memory and consciousness. Although it is often futile to trace direct influences, the relation between a particular philosophy and a certain form of art may be so intimate that the study of one in terms of the other becomes immensely rewarding.

In the case of Proust at least it is not difficult to establish even direct relationship between him and the French philosopher. A pupil of Bergson's at the Sorbonne (1891-93), and his nephew by virtue of the philosopher's marriage with his cousin Neuburger,[56] he found himself oscillating all his life between Yea and Nay.[57] In a letter to Georges de Lauris in 1909, he wrote:

"I am glad you have read some Bergson and liked him. It is as though we had been together on a great height. I don't know *L'Évolution Créatrice* . . . but I have read enough of Bergson, the parabola of his thought is already sufficiently discernible after only a single generation . . . Besides, I think I have told you of my great respect for him . . . and of the great kindness he has always shown me . . ."[58]

On the other hand, in an interview he gave to Elsie Joseph Bois, published in *Le Temps* of November 1913, he said:

"I should not in any way feel ashamed to describe my books as 'Bergsonian novels',[59] if I thought they were, for in every period, literature has tried to attach itself after the event, naturally, to the reigning philosophy. But it would not be accurate, for my work is dominated by the distinction between the 'mémoire involontaire' and 'mémoire volontaire', a distinction which is not only not to be found in M. Bergson's philosophy, but is even contradicted by it."[60]

We shall have occasion to show in a subsequent chapter

how this basis on which Proust always tried to deny Bergson's influence is refuted by the latter's clear distinction between "pure memory" and "voluntary memory".[61] But whatever be his relation with Bergson, Proust certainly renders a very faithful presentation of the Bergsonian theories of memory, *la durée* and consciousness.

Among the English writers of the first quarter of this century, we may mention T. E. Hulme who, through his various critical essays on Bergson's aesthetics and translation of *Introduction à la métaphysique*, enabled many contemporary poets and novelists to realize in Bergson an articulation of their own awareness of experience as flux. In his essay entitled "Bergson's Theory of Art", he seems to justify the impulse behind the new technique:

"The process of artistic creation would be better described as a process of discovery and disentanglement. To use the metaphor which one is now so familiar with—*the stream of inner life,* and the definite crystallized shapes on the surface—the big artist, the creative artist, the innovator, leaves the level where things are crystallized out into these definite shapes, and, diving down into *the inner flux,* comes back with a new shape which he endeavours to fix."[62]

This "new shape" is obviously a durational pattern which reveals an inner reality of things as against their crystallized surface. Therefore, although one may find oneself in this durational flux, as if one were "en présence d'une désorganisation", this is none the less reality itself.

During the last years of his life Hulme was contemplating a book on "Modern Theories of Art", a synopsis of which appears as an appendix to his *Speculations*. In the third chapter of this proposed book he planned to show how "rough analyses which artists themselves have given . . . can be interpreted in the light of new psychology—Bergson."[63] In another chapter he intended further to elaborate Bergson's theory in terms of "actual and intimate acquaintance with emotions involved—*Time and Free Will, Introduction à la Métaphysique—L'Effort Intellectual—Laughter.*"

Many other English contemporaries of Hulme felt sympathetically interested in the new philosophy. When Bergson came to the notice of the so-called "Bloomsbury Group" is not clear, but it is worth noting that Desmond MacCarthy, in a dedicatory letter to Roger Fry (dated 1914), accompanying his translation of Jules Romains's novel, *The Death of a Nobody,* drew Bergson to Fry's attention:

"At the end of the book there is an attempt to portray in the emotions of a young man walking down a rain-swept boulevard one late afternoon, a conception of the world not unlike that which M. Bergson's philosophy suggests. How far such experiences are engendered by reading M. Bergson, and how far they are independent, M. Romains can tell better."[64]

This is, however, not an essential question to ask Jules Romains or any other stream of consciousness novelist. To suggest that the new form of fiction emerged under the direct influence of Bergson would be rather misleading. In fact, Bergson was himself, like those he is supposed to have influenced, a manifestation of the *Zeitgeist.* It should, therefore, be more appropriate to say that in his philosophy one finds a most effective articulation of that intuitive sense of fluid reality of which sensitive minds were becoming aware in the early years of this century. This new realization of experience as flux manifests itself in contemporary fiction in the form of the stream of consciousness novel.

* * * * * *

William James's analysis of consciousness seems to supplement Bergson's theory of the "stream of life";[65] it may, therefore, also be helpful to understand the former's presentation of thought as a continuum.

The phrase "stream of consciousness", it may be noted, was first used by William James in *The Principles of Psychology*

(1890), and later introduced into literary criticism by May Sinclair who, in her article on Dorothy Richardson in the *Egoist* of April 1918, wrote: ". . . there is no drama, no situation, no set scene. Nothing happens. It is just life going on and on. It is Miriam's stream of consciousness, going on and on."[66]

William James, like Bergson, believes that "empty our minds as we may, some form of *changing process* remains for us to feel, and cannot be expelled."[67] Our psychic kaleidoscope is perpetually forming itself into new patterns. Like Bergson again, he exposes the Humian doctrine that our consciousness consists of discrete fragments capable of repeating themselves. On the contrary, he observes that consciousness cannot be analysed into fragments or "chopped up in bits". "Such words as 'chain' or 'train' do not describe it fitly as it presents itself in the first instance. It is nothing jointed; it flows. A 'river' or a 'stream' are the metaphors by which it is most naturally described. *In talking of it hereafter, let us call it the stream of thought, of consciousness, or of subjective life.*"[68]

In this "wonderful stream of consciousness" sensory images form the halting places or "substantive parts", and the thoughts of relations or "transitive parts" denote places of "flight". But it must be remembered that the former are mere terms of convenience and do not indicate or suggest any break in the continuous flow of consciousness, for even these "substantive parts" are invariably suffused with notions of "flight" or "movement".

Elsewhere, William James refers to the "halo or penumbra surrounding the image", "the overtone, halo or fringe",[69] suggested also by Virginia Woolf in her description of life as "a luminous halo, a semi-transparent envelope surrounding us from the beginning of consciousness to the end."[70] And when she calls upon the new writers to convey "this varying, this unknown and uncircumscribed spirit, whatever aberration or complexity it may display . . ." and, citing the example of James Joyce, asks them to "record the atoms as they fall upon the mind in the order in which they fall . . . trace the pattern, however disconnected and incoherent in appearance",[71] she defines the basic philosophical sanction behind the stream of consciousness novel.

What James calls "halo, or fringe", and Virginia Woolf "luminous halo", is nothing else than those transitional phases of our mental processes which mark the merging of the past into the present, and the fading of the present into the future, thus making experience a continuum. In James's words again, *"the knowledge of some other part of the stream, past or future, near or remote, is always mixed in with our knowledge of the present thing* . . . these lingerings of old objects, these incomings of new, are the germs of memory and expectation, the retrospective and the prospective sense of time. They give that continuity to consciousness without which it could not be called a stream."[72] It is this durational aspect of consciousness which defines the basis of the stream of consciousness novel.

We may here say a word about the present moment of experience which forms the exclusive material in the traditional novel, unless a writer chooses to introduce the past in a flashback, or what Dr. David Daiches calls "memory digression". According to the new concept of durational flux, the present loses its static nature and ceaselessly fades into the past and future. William James gives this concept a new name —"the specious present",[73] and defines it as "a bow and a stern, as it were—a rearward- and a forward-looking end."[74] In contemporary psychological fiction this specious present is always instinctively felt and sometimes directly described by novelists who employ a highly subjective, though not necessarily the stream of consciousness, technique. Gertrude Stein, for instance, calls it the "prolonged present":

"I wrote a negro story called *Melanctha*. In that there was a constant recurring and beginning there was a marked direction of being in the present although naturally I had been accustomed to past present and future, and why, because the composition forming around me was a *prolonged present*".[75]

We can easily see a certain correspondence between Gertrude Stein's and William James's conception of fluid present. Their exposition of the qualitative aspect of time, however, is not as comprehensive as that of Bergson, who remains the true embodiment of the new awareness of *durée créatrice*.

In the context of these observations, it will be seen that much new light can be thrown on the stream of consciousness form of narrative and characterization by studying it in relation to the theory of durational flux as expounded by Bergson. Interpreted in terms of *mémoire involontaire, la durée* and intuition, this kind of novel acquires a new meaning and coherence, and ceases to be "the offspring of a creator's negative mood".

In Bergson's philosophy one finds an attempt to correlate the new philosophical awareness with methods and ideals of literary composition, particularly prose-fiction. We shall now try to present in the next chapter, what may be called, "Bergson's theory of the novel", based on his observations on the novelist's art, scattered in his various philosophical writings.

Bergson's Theory of the Novel

ALTHOUGH OF ALL BERGSON'S WRITINGS, *Laughter* alone may be called a work of literary criticism, in a sense, the entire "philosophie bergsonienne est une philosophie esthétique."[1] If his theories of time, memory and consciousness evoke a response, more particularly from an artistic temperament, it is not so much due to the import of his new metaphysics as to his fundamentally aesthetic approach to life. This approach, like that of the artist, has a tendency to "put to sleep the active or rather resistant powers of our personality."[2] One of the charms of his philosophy lies in his poetic style that is rich in suggestive imagery, appropriate similes and metaphors, and a rhythmic flow of words which could have been the envy of any novelist or poet. In his lecture "Bergson and his Critique of Intellectualism", William James refers to the seductive quality of his style, "a flexibility of verbal resource that follows the thought without a crease or wrinkle, as elastic silk underclothing follows the movements of one's body . . . It is a miracle, and he is a real magician."[3]

The inherent aesthetic urges of this artist among philosophers manifest themselves in his philosophical attitudes, particularly in his attack on the conceptualization of reality.

Concepts, according to him, impede the ceaseless flow of reality, and being essentially static in nature are inherently incapable of rendering the idea of change underlying all experience. Bergson's presentation of the human situation in terms of durational continuity, *l'émotion créatrice*[4] and intuition, brings his philosophy closer to the contemporary writers and artists than to psychologists and metaphysicians.

It may, therefore, be interesting to conjecture how far a philosopher with such marked literary predilections would have been satisfied with fictional renderings of *la durée*. In a suggestive passage in *Mouvement Rétrograde du Vrai*, he recognizes though grudgingly, the efforts of certain novelists to penetrate into the thick veil of spatialized time. But have they conducted the operation methodically? Bergson here seems to make an allusion to Proust's *A La Recherche du Temps Perdu* with which he was quite familiar:

"... nous nous replacerions dans le flux de la vie intérieure, dont la philosophie ne nous paraissait retenir, trop souvent, que la congélation superficielle. Le romancier et le moraliste ne s'étaient-ils pas avancés, dans cette direction, plus loin que le philosophe? Peut-être; mais c'était par endroits seulement, sous la pression de la nécessité, qu'ils avaient brisé méthodiquement 'à la recherche du temps perdu'."[5]

Presumably, Bergson found Proust's novel, in a sense, a conceptual and therefore unmethodical representation of durational flux. The notion of *la durée* in this novel is analytically studied and formally worked into a theory of the novel towards the end of *Le Temps Retrouvé*. A real *roman fleuve,* on the other hand, would have merely presented the durational flow *methodiquement* without directing it through the channels of reason and analysis. However, the theory of time-novel as developed in this narrative is a faithful rendering of Bergson's theory of "the stream of life".

Bergson's philosophical arguments and opinions are

invariably illustrated in terms of literary forms, particularly the novel, which seems to him the most representative of them all. From his various philosophical writings one can collect enough material to form a comprehensive theory of prose-fiction. Our intention in this chapter is to study in the light of his presentation of *la durée* and memory, his theory of the novel and show how Bergsonism provides a clue to the understanding of the creative impulse behind the stream of consciousness novel, which has so far been treated in literary criticism mostly as a technical innovation.

The primary intention of the new novelist is to immerse himself completely, with a stupendous effort of the imagination, in the stream of his character's consciousness so that he ceases to have any point of view of his own. This effort of the imagination, in Bergson's terminology, may be called "intuition".[6]

According to Bergson, there are two ways of knowing reality: one adopts a point of view in relation to an object and "stops at the relative", while the other seeks an intuitive identification with the object in an effort to "possess the original". It is this realization of the original, with whatever limitations artistic representation may involve, that the stream of consciousness novelist purports to achieve. This explains how novelists like Henry James and Joseph Conrad, in spite of their extremely subjective techniques of treating character and scene, fall short of the new ideal to the extent they continue to arrange their material from a specific point of view. In the new novel, James's observer and Conrad's Marlow would be considered as remnants of the traditional novel.

Bergson, therefore, expects a psychological novelist to dispense with all intermediary stages which are only so many removes from the original. This fundamental principle of his theory of the novel, he enunciates in *An Introduction to Metaphysics*:

"Consider, again, a character whose adventures are related to me in a novel. The author may multiply the traits of his hero's character, may make him speak and act as much as he pleases, but all this can never be equivalent to the simple and indivisible feeling which I should experience if I were able for an instant to identify myself with the person of the hero himself. Out of that indivisible feeling, as from a spring, all the words, gestures and actions of the man would appear to me to flow naturally. They would no longer be accidents which, added to the idea I had formed of the character, continually enriched that idea, without ever completing it. The character would be given to me all at once, in its entirety, and the thousand incidents which manifest it, instead of adding themselves to the idea and so enriching it, would seem to me, on the contrary, to detach themselves from it, without, however, exhausting it or impoverishing its essence."[7]

Applying this test to most traditional novels one finds that whereas here there is no dearth of speech or action and the traits of the hero's character are elaborately described, yet of that "indivisible feeling" there is seldom any trace. If a character is not introduced with a full trumpeting forth of his physical and temperamental traits, the various aspects of his personality are so "faithfully" analysed that all explanatory details, instead of enriching the idea, often seem to lie heavily in so many layers over the underlying reality.

It seems that when Bergson enunciates the principle of complete identification between the artist and his subject so that he may more faithfully follow "reality in all its sinuosities", and adopt "the very movement of the inward life of things",[8] he is suggesting the possibility of something like the stream of consciousness technique which aims at giving "a direct quotation of the mind". To quote again from *An Introduction to Metaphysics,* "all the things I am told about the man provide me with so many points of view",[9] which intervene as so many veils between the consciousness and reality.

In the light of this observation, it will be seen that those critics who accuse the new novelists of lacking any point of view, only show their own incapacity to grasp the real impulse behind the new technique. In attempting to seize reality from within, with an unprecedented effort of the imagination, the new novelist ceases to have any *point de vue* in the traditional sense, as his object is to reproduce, as faithfully as possible, his character's internal rhythms of thought and experience. It is through this intuitive process that characters like Miriam Henderson, Molly Bloom, Stephen Dedalus and Mrs. Dalloway are created. All descriptive or analytical details are either completely dispensed with or reduced to a bare minimum in order to capture the "original" with "the least possible shrinkage".[10] This is precisely what Bergson means when he says "description, history and analysis leave me here in the relative. Coincidence with the person himself would alone give me the absolute."[11] Proust also implies the same aesthetic principle when he exposes the "pretension to realism" of the traditional novel:

"A literature which is content with 'describing things', with offering a wretched summary of their lines and surfaces, is, in spite of its pretension to realism, the furthest from reality . . . for it abruptly severs communication between our present self, the past of which objects retain the essence and the future in which they encourage us to search for it again."[12]

Therefore, the emergence of the stream of consciousness technique as a reaction against the traditional novel may be explained through its attempt to render reality in its original aspects. The only difference is that whereas a metaphysician may be able to realize this reality "without any expression, translation or symbolic representation", art implies, on the other hand, some sort of artificial medium without which it would not emerge into any communicable form. Bergson brings out this point very forcefully in his essay on *Laughter*:

"Could reality come into direct contact with sense and

consciousness, could we enter into immediate communion with things and with ourselves, probably art would be useless, or rather we should all be artists, for then our soul would continually vibrate in perfect accord with nature. Our eyes, aided by memory, would carve out in space and fix in time the most inimitable of pictures."[13]

But he adds that there is a veil which hangs between our consciousness and reality, and compels our senses to give us no more than "a practical simplification of reality." A true novelist would like to penetrate into the thick veil of "habit or action"[14] to grasp the individuality of things, and perceive "an entirely original harmony of forms and colours".[15] Since even language has a tendency to present all states of consciousness in crystallized forms, we fail to realize the original emotion that struggles to reach us through the refracting medium of conventional words and symbols. "When we feel love or hatred", says Bergson, "when we are gay or sad, is it really the feeling itself that reaches our consciousness with those innumerable fleeting shades of meaning and deep resounding echoes that make it something altogether our own? We should all, were it so, be novelists . . ."[16]

Our moods and sensations are queer blendings of such elements as memories impinging upon and conditioning our present sensory impressions of confused sounds, smells and sights, all forming themselves into highly fluid states of consciousness ever merging into one another. How the stream of consciousness novelist attempts to render into language some of these nuances of feeling, these "innumerable fleeting shades of meaning and deep resounding echoes", in order to capture "the emotion, the original mood . . . in its undefiled essence",[17] may be seen from the following passage:

"The cook whistled in the kitchen. She heard the click of the typewriter. It was her life, and, bending her head over the hall table, she bowed beneath the influence, felt blessed and purified, saying to herself, *as she took the pad* with the telephone message on it, how moments like this are buds on the tree of life, flowers of darkness they are, she thought (as if some lovely rose had blossomed for her eyes only); not for a moment did she believe in God; but all the more, she thought, *taking up the pad*, must one repay in daily life to servants, yes, to dogs and canaries, above all to Richard her husband, who was the foundation of it—of the gay sounds, of the green lights, of the cook even whistling, for Mrs. Walker was Irish and whistled all day long—one must pay back from this secret deposit of exquisite moments, she thought, *lifting the pad*, while Lucy stood by her trying to explain how 'Mr. Dalloway, ma'am'——!"[18]

Between the taking of the pad with the telephone message on it and Lucy's explanation of it, Virginia Woolf has here suggested "innumerable fleeting shades" of various other strands of consciousness which coalesce into this larger sensation—the receiving of a message from her husband, Richard Dalloway. This sensation is repeated three times in the passage as if it were a refrain or a *leit-motif* into which cohere qualitatively such heterogeneous elements as the whistling of the cook, the clicking of the typewriter, the gay sounds, the green lights, etc. How much richer this single moment of experience has been made by a blending together of this multitude of "overtones, haloes and shadows", to borrow from William James's terminology, may be realized from the fact that a traditional novelist would have contented himself with a mere description of the simple act of lifting the pad, without suggesting any of these "fleeting shades".

Let us now consider an extract from Molly Bloom's monologue in which she recalls one of her earlier experiences before marriage:

". . . the night we missed the boat at Algeciras the watchman going about serene with his lamp and O that awful deepdown torrent O and the sea the sea crimson sometimes like fire and the glorious sunsets and the figtrees in the

Alameda gardens yes and all the queer little streets and pink
and blue and yellow houses and the rosegardens and the
jessamine and geraniums and cactuses and Gibraltar as a girl
where I was a Flower of the mountain yes when I put the rose
in my hair like the Andalusian girls used or shall I wear a red
yes and how he kissed me under the Moorish wall . . ."[19]

Here again the memory of the kiss, symbolizing Molly
Bloom's affirmation of life, flows into her consciousness, borne
on the stream of her thought which overflows with a symphonic
cumulation of a rich blending of colours and flowers. "The sea
crimson sometimes like fire . . . pink and blue and yellow
houses" set, as it were, against a resplendent opulence of "the
glorious sunsets", which merge into the red rose, signifying
complete surrender of the lonely spirit to the great sea, that
is love and life.

It may also be seen from these extracts how the impediment of language to the smooth flow of consciousness is
acutely felt by these novelists. Hence their attempt to break
through this barrier by employing a highly fluid syntactical
construction of sentences to evoke the original emotion in all
its complexity. *L'émotion créatrice,* as it may be more appropriately called, is the ideal before these writers who are not
satisfied with merely describing things but would "delve yet
deeper still. Beneath these joys and sorrows . . . they grasp . . .
certain rhythms of life and breath that are closer to man than
his inmost feelings, being the living law—varying with each
individual . . . By setting free and emphasizing this music, they
force it upon our attention; they compel us, willy-nilly, to
fall in with it, like passers-by who join in a dance."[20]

In these words Bergson has aptly described the response of
the reader to a stream of consciousness narrative like Dorothy
Richardson's *Pilgrimage* or Molly Bloom's monologue. And
again when he pleads for a "certain immateriality of life" in
art, and a brushing aside of "the conventional and socially
accepted generalities",[21] he could have referred to the

Edwardian novelists who are labelled by Virginia Woolf as *materialists*. In fact, she indirectly justifies her own technique, and Bergson's theory of the novel when she says: "In contrast with those whom we have called materialists, Mr. Joyce is spiritual; he is concerned at all costs to reveal the flickerings of that innermost flame which flashes its messages through the brain, and in order to preserve it he disregards with complete courage whatever seems to him adventitious, whether it be probability, or coherence, or any other of these signposts which for generations have served to support the imagination of a reader when called upon to imagine what he can neither touch nor see."[22]

Let us next consider what becomes of personality when we brush aside "the conventional and socially accepted generalities", and try to penetrate into the depth of the human soul. "There is one reality, at least", observes Bergson, "which we all seize from within, by intuition and not by simple analysis. It is our own personality in its flowing through time— our self which endures."[23] This fundamental self is comparatively ignored by the traditional novelist in favour of the conventional ego, which is a mere conglomeration of perceptions, memories, tendencies and motor habits laid out in a clearly demarcated spatial or chronological sequence. These elements of psychic life have served the traditional novelist faithfully, being always at his beck and call to explain consistency in character. The new novelist, however, borne along the current of new philosophical and psychological trends, finds himself confronted with a fluid aspect of human personality which refuses to lend itself to any logical analysis.

* * * * * *

In memory alone is the self continuous and becomes a flowing river of consciousness. Memory, being a conditioning factor in all our mental processes, constitutes the essence of the stream of consciousness novel. Bergson, again, analyses this phenomenon not only from a metaphysical point of view but also from an aesthetic angle, particularly basing his analysis on the novelist's handling of it. In order to understand his criticism of the treatment of memory in the traditional novel, let us first go into his assessment of the importance of memory in our consciousness.

To begin with, perception itself is never unmixed with memories as "the formation of memory is never posterior to the formation of perception: it is contemporaneous with it."[24] In *Matter and Memory* Bergson observes that "with the immediate and present data of our senses we mingle a thousand details out of our past experience. In most cases these memories supplant our actual perceptions, of which we then retain only a few hints, thus using them merely as 'signs' that recall to us former images.[25] Even the length of a perception does not in the least alter this character, for "however brief we suppose any perception to be, it always occupies a certain duration, and involves consequently an effort of memory which prolongs one into another a plurality of moments."[26] It is this perpetual lengthening shadow of memories over our present experience that blurs the boundaries between the past, present and future, for what else is the present if not "the invisible progress of the past gnawing into the future?"[27]

Bergson further distinguishes between two different forms of memory—*mémoire involontaire* and *mémoire volontaire*. Whereas the latter is the creature of reason and will, supplying only those images from the past which are conducive to practical living, the former has no such utilitarian significance as "it stores up the past by the mere necessity of its own nature."[28] To the creative artist, the first form of memory, *mémoire involontaire,* alone has any aesthetic "use" for it forms the raw material of art.[29] Bergson calls it "mémoire par excellence" and affirms its supremacy over mere "learnt recollections", because it is "perfect from the outset; time can add nothing to its image without disfiguring it."[30] In a sense, it is eternal and derives its validity from the reality itself and not from the intellectualized ways of thinking, developed and perfected by man to assist him in his daily living. "This spontaneous recollection, which is masked by the acquired recollection, may flash out at intervals; but it disappears at the least movement of voluntary memory."[31] Its ways are *capricious*,[32] its flow uncertain and it waylays our reason and consciousness to reveal, as it were, in a flash some obscure depth of our soul. It is through this *souvenir involontaire* that the new novelist tries to convey a sense of reality that is both vital and dynamic, and whose wings have not been dried to adorn the notebook of a botanist. *Mémoire involontaire* thus forms the essence of the new psychological fiction, for in it alone one can find a perfect blending of the past and present.

Surprisingly enough, even in the face of this clear distinction between the two forms of memory, Proust still chooses to assert repeatedly his claims to be the first to distinguish between voluntary and involuntary memory,[33] and more particularly to emphasize the importance of the latter to a creative artist. It is equally surprising how almost all critics have supported his claim against Bergson's without caring to ascertain for themselves the validity of his repeated assertions.[34]

In a letter to René Blum, Proust writes about *Matter and Memory*: "It is an extremely real book, but supported after a fashion by a peduncle of reminiscences to imitate involuntary memory (which in my opinion, although *Bergson does not make this distinction*, is the only valid one; intellectual and visual memory gives us only inexact facsimiles of the past, which no more resemble it than pictures by bad painters resemble the spring . . ."[35]

In another letter to his friend Antoine Bibesco, Proust attempts further to elaborate his position: ". . . My work is dominated by a distinction which not only doesn't figure in

Bergson's philosophy but which is even contradicted by it."[36] Voluntary memory, he adds, "which is above all the memory of the intelligence end of the eyes, gives us only the surface of the past without the truth; but when an odour, a taste, rediscovered under entirely different circumstances evoke for us, in spite of ourselves, the past, we sense how different is this past from the one we thought we remembered and which our voluntary memory was painting like a bad painter using false colours . . .

"I believe that it is involuntary memories practically altogether that the artist should call for the primary subject matter of his work. First, just because they are involuntary, because they can take shape of their own accord, inspired by the resemblance to an identical minute, they alone have the stamp of authenticity. Then they bring things back to us in an exact proportion of memory and of forgetting."[37]

Although this is a clear statement of the importance of involuntary memory to an artist, Proust shows his lack of understanding of Bergson's philosophy when he says that the distinction is "even contradicted by it". On the contrary, both Bergson and Proust show a very close resemblance in their analysis and assessment of *souvenir involontaire*. One may, however, trace some difference in their approach to this phenomenon. Proust believes that the present sensation, an odour or a taste, by virtue of some associated link, enables us to *ascend* into the region of "pure memory" which then unfolds to our minds the entire past with all its details preserved in their nascent state. According to Bergson, on the other hand, the present moment of experience by some associated link makes the entire region of "pure memory" *descend* in response to its appeal, passive or active. But it will be seen that he also presents more or less the same view, only reversing the terms of this analysis. In either sense, the mind establishes contact with the entire range of our past experience. Although it is only during certain heightened states of perception that we become more consciously aware of our perpetual link with the past, the link subsists, all the same, in all our mental processes. Bergson affirms this fact when he says: "Yes, I believe our past life is there, preserved even to the minutest details; nothing is forgotten; all we have perceived, thought, willed, from the first awakening of our consciousness, persists indefinitely."[38]

"We know, for instance," he writes, "when we read a psychological novel, that certain associations of ideas there depicted for us are true, that they may have been lived; others offend us, or fail to give us an impression of reality, because we feel in them the effect of a connexion, mechanically and artificially brought about, between different mental levels, as though the author had not taken care to maintain himself on that plane of the mental life which he had chosen."[39]

Bergson has been speaking of two different planes of consciousness: of action and dream. Whereas on the former plane our recollections invariably converge on the immediate course of action we want to adopt, on the latter plane "pure memory" or *mémoire involontaire* "with the totality of our past, is continually pressing forward, so as to insert the largest possible part of itself into the present action."[40] Corresponding to these two planes of awareness are "two different mental *dispositions* . . . two distinct degrees of tension of the memory",[41] the one more disposed to action, the other nearer to the pure image.

Although Bergson admits that it is a difficult problem to discover the principles underlying these two different tensions of memory, it is imperative for a psychological novelist—"the painter of mental scenery"—(as he calls him) not to confound them. A stream of consciousness novelist can avoid this confusion, if he succeeds in achieving complete identification with his character's flow of consciousness. A traditional novelist, on the other hand, compelled to arrange his material within a rigid framework, is more prone to this confusion.

By adopting such devices as "memory digressions", he brings into an artificial juxtaposition with the present moment of experience a great mass of edited and modified associated ideas and images from the past. Whereas such a method may serve for clarity or easy communication, it does not always present a convincing picture of our mental life, because we often feel in such juxtapositions "the effect of a connexion, mechanically and artificially brought about."

Since the association of ideas is, as Bergson also admits, [42] a fundamental basis of the stream of consciousness, we may here inquire into this aspect of the new technique. We need not investigate into the laws of association—whatever they be—our exclusive concern being to show that they make experience a continuum, a ceaseless flow of retrospect and prospect.

It was John Locke who first used the term "association of ideas" in his *Essay Concerning Human Understanding*". [43] His thesis was that given simple ideas as elements, we could form complex ideas out of them. Similar theories of association were held by numerous British philosophers in the eighteenth and nineteenth centuries, and though there is an occasional suggestion of a more Bergsonian position (as in Thomas Brown's discussion of the *"spontaneous chemistry of the mind"* [44]), on the whole, all these philosophers, up to and including Mill and Bain, were guilty of what, in Bergson's view, was the mistake of intellectualizing impressions rather than treating them as they really are in actual experience. Any attempt to analyse feelings or ideas, says Bergson in *Time and Free Will*, would be a move away from a truer representation of reality, because "the feeling itself is a being which lives and develops and is therefore constantly changing . . ." [45] Our emotions grow in a "duration whose moments permeate one another. By separating these moments from each other, by spreading out time in space", [46] we cause our emotions to lose their true life and colour.

A true novelist, according to Bergson, should be primarily concerned with bringing out the inner relation between things. He should attempt to present our ideas and feelings in their nascent freshness, by dispensing with all intervening layers between our consciousness and reality. The novelist must take the reader below the neatly arranged surface of our consciousness and show there a multitude of secondary impressions impinging upon the present moment of experience. This is what the stream of consciousness novelist purports to achieve by employing a highly fluid form of narrative. In a passage which defines one of the main features of his theory of the novel, Bergson says:

"Now, if some bold novelist, tearing aside the cleverly woven curtain of our conventional ego, shows us under this appearance of logic a fundamental absurdity, under this juxtaposition of simple states an infinite permeation of a thousand different impressions which have already ceased to exist the instant they are named, we commend him for having known us better than we knew ourselves."[47]

This is, however, not the case with most traditional novelists whose presentation of character is confined mainly to the "conventional ego" arranged in a chronological sequence. This method of character-portrayal seldom admits the reader into what may be called the durational undercurrents of human personality. The stream of consciousness novelist, on the other hand, being mainly concerned with portraying personality "in its flowing through time", feels the necessity of penetrating into the thick curtain of our superficial self and presenting nascent states of consciousness as permeating one another in a process of creative renewal. To "name" or clothe any of these fleeting impressions in words or images is a difficult task indeed, but this kind of novelist shows his "boldness" in suggesting a sense of fluidity through various ingenious linguistic devices. His delineation of character is, therefore, "bold" and dramatic. In Leopold

Bloom's character, for instance, we are made to realize through the meanderings of his consciousness, the inner reality of his self. And similarly as we float along Miriam Henderson's stream of thought, we become aware of "an infinite permeation of a thousand impressions" which reveal the pattern of her consciousness as it melts from one state into another.

The stream of consciousness novelist thus attempts to present symbolically "this creation of self by self", [48] this continuous "swelling" [49] which defines the true nature of all our mental processes. Our thoughts and emotions are, in a sense, living organisms. The aesthetic problem before the new novelist is how to catch thought in its vital nascent state and make it pass, still living, into the soul of another. In a passage in "The Soul and the Body", Bergson elaborates his concept of "the living thought" as the basis of all successful psychological fiction. Speaking in terms of his "bold" novelist, he observes:

"The harmony he seeks is a certain correspondence between the comings and goings of his mind and the phrasing of his speech, a correspondence so perfect that *the waves of his thought, borne by the sentence, stir us sympathetically,* and the words, taken individually no longer count: there is nothing left but the flow of meaning which runs through the words, *nothing but two minds* which, *without intermediary*, seem to vibrate directly in unison with one another. The rhythm of speech has here, then, no other object than that of reproducing the rhythm of the thought: and what can the rhythm of the thought be but the rhythm of the scarcely conscious nascent movements which accompany it?" [50]

The unprecedented extent to which the stream of consciousness novelist has succeeded in representing his characters' nascent "waves of thought", and seeking complete identification with his subject "without any intermediary" is manifest from such characters as Molly Bloom and Miriam

Henderson. By means of a prodigious effort of the imagination, the new novelist attempts to immerse himself in his character's stream of thought to represent its "real, concrete" nature.

*   *   *   *   *   *

Language, according to Bergson, is an instrument of the intelligence, a crystallization of mobile thoughts and emotions. Words are only lifeless and static representations of a reality that is perpetually growing and changing into new forms. But unless one could attain to a mystic identification with the object,[51] words remain the only inevitable medium of communication. A bold novelist, however, urged by a genuine creative impulse, can evoke a sense of fluid reality by dissociating words, as far as possible, from their traditional context and employing them in new arrangements and combinations. Such a novelist obviously reverses the traditional method of writing by "working back from the intellectual and social plane to a point in the soul from which there springs an imperative demand for creation . . . *To obey it completely new words would have to be coined,* new ideas would have to be created, but this would no longer be communicating something, it would not be writing. *Yet the writer will attempt to realize the unrealizable.*"[52]

Dorothy Richardson, Virginia Woolf, and more particularly James Joyce, are essentially engaged in this attempt to "realize the unrealizable", to break through the meshes of the conventional word and penetrate into the durational aspect of experience. To establish the continuity of durational flux, these novelists employ all kinds of linguistic devices such as a frequent use of parenthesis, prepositional participles, co-ordinative conjunctions, the imperfect tense, dots, etc. To render a few illustrations:

(a) *Parenthesis*

"Parrots shrieking break the intense stillness of the jungle.

4

(Here the trams start.) The swallow dips her wings in midnight pools. (Here we talk.)"[53]

"Now people who make a single impression, and that, in the main, a good one (for there seems to be a virtue in simplicity), are those who keep their equilibrium in midstream. (I instantly see fish with their noses one way, the stream rushing past another.)"[54]

(b) *Prepositional use of participles*

"Straightening himself and stealthily fingering his pocketknife he started after her to follow this woman . . ."[55]

"But Rezia Warren Smith cried, walking down Harley Street, that she did not like that man."[56]

(c) *Co-ordinative Conjunctions*

In the style of Virginia Woolf, there is a marked tendency to introduce new paragraphs with co-ordinative conjunctions, particularly "for" and "and", in order to indicate the uninterrupted flow of consciousness from one paragraph to another. For instance,

"*And* really Clarissa's eyes filled with tears. Her mother, walking in a garden! *But* alas, she must go.

For there was Professor Brierly, who lectured on Milton, talking to little Jim Hutton (who was unable even for a party like this to compass both tie and waistcoat or make his hair lie flat), *and* even at this distance they were quarrelling, she could see. *For* Professor Brierly was a very queer fish."[57]

(d) *The Imperfect Tense*

The predominant tense in the stream of consciousness narrative is not the preterite as in Dickens, Thackeray and Wells, but the imperfect:

"The room was waking up from its letter-writing. People were moving about."[58]

(e) *Dots*

"Adam was like a German . . . English too . . . Impudent bombastic creature . . . a sort of man who would call his wife 'my dear'."[59]

Thus an analysis of any passage from a stream of consciousness novel would show how an attempt to render, what may be called, Bergsonian *durée* inevitably involves these writers in a radical dislocation of normal prose syntax.

Joyce goes even a step further by completely disregarding the normal syntax ("Stuck on the pane two flies buzzed, stuck."[60]), and making copious additions to the English vocabulary.[61] Impelled by an urge to make words express "Change" and not merely "the Form",[62] he ends up by using in *Finnegans Wake* an altogether new language of his own invention. Thus language that is partial to rectilinear deduction is remoulded to represent becoming.

But whatever the devices employed by Joyce and other stream of consciousness novelists, their fundamental intention is to make words perform the function of "fluid concepts" and thus represent experience as a process. In other words, the new method of literary composition implies, in terms of Bergsonian metaphysics, not a mere combination of pre-existing concepts, but an emergence of ever new concepts from a "direct and lived intuition".

If Dorothy Richardson,[63] Virginia Woolf,[64] and James Joyce[65] had in mind a certain theory of fiction as exemplified in their work, so was Bergson evolving a similar theory of the novel,[66] corresponding to his philosophical theories of *la durée, mémoire involontaire,* aesthetic intuition, *l'émotion créatrice* and *le langage dynamique.* His utterances on the novelist's art are scattered in his various philosophical writings. How closely the main elements of his philosophy are reflected in the stream of consciousness novel may now be seen from an examination of the work of Dorothy Richardson, Virginia Woolf and James Joyce.

CHAPTER **3**

Dorothy Richardson

"HIS WHOLE UNDERTAKING", WRITES DOROTHY
Richardson about Proust, "the reduction of phenomena to
their laws—the laws, that is to say, of science and psychology
to date as taught for him, by Huxley and by Bergson—was, in
his view, man's only way of escape from life's pain."[1]

With certain reservations this would be as accurate an
assessment of her own work as that of Proust. However,
unlike him, she is not so much concerned with reducing
"phenomena to their laws" as with merely presenting them
with a minimum of critical analysis. But as with her French
contemporary, it is philosophic rather than scientific thought
which defines the tone of her narrative. Bergson's thought
seems to be as much the distinguishing feature of *À la recherche
du temps perdu* as of *Pilgrimage,* for the entire work of Dorothy
Richardson bears a very close resemblance to his theories of
la durée and "pure memory".

The question of direct influence, as suggested earlier, is
always gross and palpable, and Dorothy Richardson herself
denies any deliberate borrowings from Bergson's philosophy.

"I was never consciously aware of any specific influence
. . .", she writes in a letter to this author. "No doubt Bergson

36

influenced many minds, if only by putting into words something then dawning within the human consciousness: an increased sense of the inadequacy of the clock as a time-measurer."[2]

The process of literary creation, individual and mysterious as it always is, can seldom be discussed in terms of "direct influences". Nevertheless, it sometimes does help to discover certain recognizable threads in a literary mosaic with a view to understanding more successfully the basic intention of a writer. Dorothy Richardson was certainly not consciously influenced by the French philosopher in evolving a fluid medium of expression. If in the early stages of Miriam's pilgrimage, she felt herself following "the lonely track"[3], she must have soon after discovered in Bergson a kindred spirit who enabled her to render a more detailed presentation of the phenomena of time and memory.

Bergson's appeal to the imaginative writer lies primarily in his *literary treatment*[4] of an intuitive perception of reality as a ceaseless movement of change. Round him, as round a central thread, were crystallizing into definite modes of thought and expression, all those minds who experienced a similar realization.

Apart from any direct acquaintance with Bergson's thought, Dorothy Richardson's interest in the new philosophy might have been sympathetically aroused through three possible channels: Proust, the Symbolists and May Sinclair.

Proust's work, as we have already suggested, is the best introduction to Bergson's thought and Dorothy Richardson recognizes him as the first adventurer in the new path. "News came from France of one Marcel Proust", she writes in her preface to *Pilgrimage,* "said to be producing an unprecedented profound and opulent reconstruction of experience focused from within the mind of a single individual, and, since Proust's first volume had been published and several others written by 1913, the France of Balzac now appeared to have produced the earliest adventurer."[5]

In both these novelists the narrative comes nearest to a withdrawal from external phenomena and an absorption in introspective musings, making the novel reflective and episodic. Goethe, whom Dorothy Richardson presents as another exponent of the psychological novel, expounds a similar theory in *Wilhelm Meister*:

"In the novel, reflections and incidents should be featured; in drama, character and action. The novel must proceed slowly, and *the thought-processes of the principal figure must,* by one device or another, *hold up the development of the whole* . . . The hero of the novel must be acted upon, or, at any rate, not himself the principal operator."[6]

Interpreted in Bergsonian terms, this "manifesto" would require a novelist, privileged to work on a wider canvas and in a more fluid medium than a dramatist, to reveal "the thought-processes" of his characters engaged in ceaseless becoming. If the leading characters in a novel, according to Goethe, should be "retarding personalities", it is because character does not progress along a chronological sequence of events but evolves through a creative duration that flows both backward and forward. It is in presenting this Bergsonian view of personality and time that Dorothy Richardson comes close to Proust. There are obvious points of resemblance between *Pilgrimage* and *À la recherche du temps perdu*. Both are Bergsonian "remembrances of things past" and, divided into twelve parts, are pilgrimages through *la durée* rather than space.

Another link with Bergsonism may be traced through contemporary French symbolists and other writers who showed a marked influence of Bergson on their work.[7] It is worth noting here that Dorothy Richardson's genius is essentially poetic with a strong leaning towards the symbolist mode of expression.[8] Her basic intention is to render life not in terms of distinct outlines but in terms of fleeting

impressions. A typical passage from *Honeycomb* may show how
she strikes one as a symbolist poet writing fluid prose:

"The West End street . . . flags of pavement flowing . . .
sliding into each other . . . I am part of the dense smooth
clean paving stone . . . sunlit; gleaming under dark winter
rain . . . dark and light . . . dawn, stealing . . . Life streamed
up from the close dense stone . . . glinting transparencies of
mauve and amber and green, rose-pearl and milky blue,
welded to a flowing tide, freshening and flowing through her blood,
a sea rising and falling with her breathing."[9]

In this passage she clearly makes an effort to render life
in terms of fluid impressions—flowing, rising and falling,
making words convey more than their expository meaning in
a true symbolist manner.[10]

Another possible mediator between Dorothy Richardson
and Bergsonism could have been May Sinclair, who is not only
a novelist but also a philosopher of some talent. A close
literary associate of Miss Richardson's, she was one of the first
to introduce *Pilgrimage* to the public in an article she wrote in
the *Egoist* of April 1918.[11] In the early decades of this century
she was expounding her own theory of "new idealism"[12]
which, in spite of a different terminology, bears an intimate
resemblance to Bergson's dynamism. Even where she succeeds
in pointing out certain flaws in Bergson's time-philosophy, the
novelist in her succumbs to the philosopher's influence.
"Discovering dilemmas in M. Bergson's philosophy", she
writes in her preface to *A Defence of Idealism,* "is an enthralling
occupation while you are about it but it leaves no solid
satisfaction behind. It does not, as Samuel Butler would have
said, give you 'peace at the last'. When it is all over you feel
as if it had not been quite worth while. What do a few logical
dilemmas more or less matter in the work of a poet and a
seer? . . . To try to analyse it, to break through that texture
of beautiful imagination, is to lay violent hands on a living,
palpitating thing."[13]

Although we have above attempted to suggest certain possible links of relationship between Dorothy Richardson and Bergson, it must be emphatically repeated that she was not influenced by him. These direct or indirect contacts with Bergsonism were merely in the nature of a self-realization which enabled her to discover herself as yet another manifestation of the *Zeitgeist*. It would, therefore, be more appropriate to discuss her work as an example of parallelism between the stream of consciousness technique and the Bergsonian flux.

* * * * * *

To Dorothy Richardson, although a minor novelist as compared with Virginia Woolf and James Joyce, is due the credit of being the earliest English novelist to make a consistent use of the stream of consciousness method. Katherine Mansfield is perhaps the only other English writer who, as early as 1908, was groping for a similar method of revealing the inner flux. One finds a clear indication of this new thrust towards inner reality in her first short-story, *The Tiredness of Rosabel*. The heroine of this story, Rosabel, bears a marked resemblance to Miriam Henderson. They are both highly sensitive and introspective characters, revealing through transparent consciousness their inner process of becoming. A passage each from Katherine Mansfield's *The Tiredness of Rosabel* and Dorothy Richardson's *Dark Tunnel* may illustrate this point:

"As she swung on to the step of the Atlas bus, grabbed her skirt with one hand and clung to the railing with the other, Rosabel thought . . . there was a sickening smell of warm humanity . . . everybody had the same expression, sitting so still, staring in front of them . . . She was glad to reach Richmond Road, but from the corner of the street until she came to No. 26 she thought of those four flights of stairs. Oh, why four flights!"[14]

"She found the dark green Atlas bus standing ready by the kerb and waited till it was about to start . . . and then jumped hurriedly in . . . Securing an empty corner she sat down provisionally . . . her eyes, turned inwards on splendours . . . Everyone was invisible and visionless, united in the spectacle, gilding and hiding the underworld in a brilliant embroidery . . . Baker Street began all right; one felt safe going up Orchard Street, past the beautiful china shop and the Romish richness of Burns and Oates . . ."[15]

These passages illustrate, in Bergson's terminology, a constant interpenetration of different states of consciousness into one another. It is obvious that Katherine Mansfield also feels, like Dorothy Richardson, the necessity of breaking through the hard crust of outer experience in an attempt to represent the inner flow of thought. She differs from Dorothy Richardson in degree not kind, her canvas being more restricted and her use of the fluid technique not as consistent.

Dorothy Richardson alone, therefore, deserves the credit of making consistent use of a new medium which presents personality as a process and not a state.[16] Her contribution to the English novel was rightly recognized by many contemporary critics who saw in her method an opening for new possibilities. Among her early admirers were Rebecca West, Frank Swinnerton, Hugh Walpole, and Wells who remarked that her novels "mark an epoch in the technical development of the novelist's art, a real and successful thrust towards a new reality and intensity of rendering that has exerted a powerful influence upon a multitude of contemporary writers . . ."[17]

* * * * * *

Flux, in the strict Bergsonian sense, is the defining feature of the entire work of Dorothy Richardson. Hypo, Michael, Amabel, Eleanor Dear, Densley, Harriett and Eve are all conceived through Miriam's fluid consciousness which, like a sensitive filament, is perpetually quivering, recording the slightest fluctuation in the environment. We see "all things *sub specie durationis*",[18] making the entire narrative look like a symphony that swells into larger dimensions as it progresses through various movements. We realize, through Miriam's intuitive experience of life, the "vision of universal becoming"[19] from *Pointed Roofs,* the opening chapter of this long "chronicle", to *Dimple Hill* which enables her to enjoy peaceful rest, amidst idyllic surroundings, in involuntary recapitulation of the past. And yet it may be remembered that even *Dimple Hill* with its inconsequential character is not an ending (how could there be any conclusion in a real process of becoming?) but only a phase in the stream of life that flows on indefinitely. In fact, Dorothy Richardson did again take up the link and published some further parts of *Pilgrimage* under the title "Work in Progress" and again left the "concluding" parts as inconclusive as any of the preceding "chapters".[20] *Pilgrimage,* therefore, is a true symbol of that imperceptible process of eternal becoming that marks our ceaseless reactions to phenomena, dramatic or singularly "ordinary" and "dull". This psychic biography of Miriam Henderson, covers a range of about fourteen years and such different places as Hanover, Banbury, Newlands, London, Oberland and Dimple Hill, presenting, as it were symbolically, the stream of life flowing on and on.

And yet Miriam Henderson's mind sometimes allows the "meddling intellect" to overshadow the vision of becoming, which her intuitive self persistently conjures up. She then begins to feel the great necessity of "supports" or "fixed points" in the moving wheel of experience. This aesthetic dilemma is very adequately summed up by Bergson in *The Creative Mind*:

"Before the spectacle of this universal mobility there may be some who will be seized with dizziness. They are accustomed to *terra firma*; they cannot get used to the rolling and pitching. They must have 'fixed' points to which they can attach thought and existence. They think that if everything passes, nothing exists; and that if reality is mobility, it has already ceased to exist at the moment one thinks it—it eludes thought. The material world, they say, is going to disintegrate, and the mind will drown in the torrent-like flow of things.—Let them be reassured! Change, if they consent to look directly at it without an interposed veil, will very quickly appear to them to be the most substantial and durable thing possible."[21]

So long as Miriam Henderson relies on her intuitive faculty she does not look for any *terra firma*, and accepts unreservedly the "torrent-like flow of things". It is only when she looks at the phenomenon of flux through the refracting medium of intellect that she finds herself caught inextricably between the two conflicting and irreconcilable views of reality—being and becoming. In such moments the intellectual aspect of her personality dominates her entire self and makes her feel the necessity of discovering some "fixed points", to which contraries could be conveniently referred. Pressed under this urge to resolve experience into static intelligible symbols, Miriam Henderson leans towards "being" as an all-satisfying principle underlying reality. This tendency towards conceptualizing experience finds expression in *Clear Horizon* where Miriam prepares herself even to give up her relationship with Hypo, because he would not accept "being" as the only impregnable and irrefutable view of reality.

"Vanity, too, had helped. If it were vanity to hope that she herself might be instrumental in changing his views. Yet she knew that she would gladly sacrifice his companionship and all that depended therefrom for the certainty of seeing his world of ceaseless 'becoming' exchanged for one wherein should be included also the fact of 'being', the overwhelming, smiling hint, proof against all possible tests, provided by the mere existence of anything, anywhere."[22]

Miriam would be satisfied only if Hypo could also embrace "being" as a significant aspect of "becoming", but soon after she gives up even this compromising attitude to accept *being* as the only ultimate reality, and *becoming* as its extraneous concomitant with no exclusive identity of its own.

"Being versus becoming. Becoming versus being. Look after the being and the becoming will look after itself. Look after the becoming and the being will look after itself? Not so certain. Therefore it is certain that becoming depends upon being.[23] Man carries his bourne within himself and is there already, or he would not even know that he exists."[24]

This shows how on the dialectical plane Dorothy Richardson falls in with the traditional metaphysical emphasis on "being" as against "ceaseless flux". This passage is more definite and assertive and not as non-committal as the one quoted earlier. Of the two contraries, becoming and being, the former depends upon the latter because it is "not so certain" that "being" will look after itself if "becoming" is well taken care of. Whereas "being" is finite and immutable, "becoming" loses itself in a haze of continual change. And in presenting personality as carrying its "bourne" within itself, she moves still further away from Bergson who believes in a creative evolution of self towards unpredictable and unforeseeable forms.

But we have noted earlier that this vacillation and subsequent affirmation of *being* as the only reality is merely a passing phase of Miriam's awareness and does not represent her fundamental attitude. This dilemma exists only on the dialectical plane, for as soon as Miriam stops conceptualizing she realizes *becoming,* in the strict Bergsonian sense, as the only true explanation of experience. There is then a shift from an intellectual reconstruction of experience as a state to an intuitive realization of it as a process. This process of creative becoming, in which her self is involved ever since she leaves her home to take up various careers, is described in a passage in *Dimple Hill*:

"And even now, though she could imagine herself built into Fräulein Pfaff's school, tolerantly collaborating with her in handling successive drafts of girls from prosperous English families and, in the end, taking over the school herself; or staying deedily on with the Pernes and *becoming*, at last, approximately, a modern Perne; or even staying with the Corries until she had learned their world and *become a flexible part of it* . . ."[25]

It is obvious how each fresh experience presses her gently into a new kaleidoscopic pattern. These different careers may not appear to be dramatic and soul-making in the traditional sense, yet their impress on her growing self is, none the less, so indelibly marked that after each experience she is never her old self again, and the stream of her becoming flows on now turbid, now clear, to an unforeseen and unforeseeable destination. "*Not things made*", observes Bergson, "*but things in the making,* not self-maintaining states, but only changing states, exist . . . The consciousness we have of our own self in its continual flux introduces us to the interior of a reality . . ."[26] Dorothy Richardson, like other stream of consciousness novelists, does not attempt to regularize this life-flow into any definite channels. It is in her analysis of Wilson's character in *Dawn's Left Hand* that she clearly brings out this conception of personality:

"He was two people. A man achieving, becoming, driving forward to *unpredictable becomings,* delighting in the process, devoting himself, compelling himself, whom so frankly he criticized and so genuinely deplored, to *a ceaseless becoming,* ceaseless assimilating of anything that promised to serve the interests of a ceaseless becoming for life as he saw it."[27]

Human personality, "driving forward to unpredictable becomings", is, however, as true of Miriam's own character as of Hypo's. This process of "ceaseless becoming" reveals itself through Miriam's stream of consciousness which reflects the fugitive sensory impressions of the present as perpetually recreated by memories.

* * * * * *

The stream of consciousness technique as employed by Dorothy Richardson is a novel method of representing this conception of dynamic personality and she remains its most literal exponent. But it is surprising to note that she has never taken kindly to the use of the term "stream of consciousness". In an article on "Novels" she describes the label as a "lamentably ill-chosen metaphor . . . still, in literary criticism, pursuing its foolish way."[28] Again in her preface to *Pilgrimage* she makes an ironical reference to the use of this term. "Phrases began to appear, formulae devised to meet the exigencies of literary criticism. 'The Stream of Consciousness' lyrically led the way, to be gladly welcomed by all who could persuade themselves of the possibility of comparing consciousness to a stream."[29]

No doubt, all literary labels are mere terms of convenience and need not be taken too seriously in their literal implications. Dorothy Richardson suggests "fountain of consciousness"[30] as a more appropriate metaphor. Although a "fountain" may signify more contemplative intensity than mere surface-flow, the new label also does not seem to be a happier choice. The fact that *Pilgrimage* is still an endless "stream of consciousness going on and on", is evident not only from the extremely fluid and indeterminate form of narrative employed by Dorothy Richardson, but also from her innumerable allusions, both direct and oblique, to consciousness as a flowing stream. To quote only a few examples:

"He paused, gravely consulting her face; she made no effort to withhold the wave of anger flowing out over the words that stood mocking her on the desolate air, a bridge, carrying them up over *the stream of her mind* and forward, leaving her communications behind for ever."[31] (*Deadlock*)

In a passage in *Clear Horizon* she refers to the quick succession of thoughts in our mental processes: "Into the rising tide of discomfort flowed *the stream of Amabel's silent communications* . . . the swiftness of the mental processes

reflected within it."[32] Occasionally we also have little eddies
in Miriam's stream of consciousness: "She sat in a lively
misery, following the whirling circle of thoughts round and
round, stabbed by their dull thorns . . ."[33] Her awareness of
the present is always tinged with "scenes from the future,
moving in boundless backgrounds . . . streaming unsummoned
into her mind".[34] To the highly introspective mind of
Miriam even the roads look "like long thoughts . . . going on
and on".[35] Whenever she takes up a book to read, she becomes
aware of a sense of dynamic contact between her mind and
the author: "the strange currents, which came whenever she
was alone and at ease flowing to the tips of her fingers, seemed
to flow into the book as she held it and to be met and
satisfied."[36]

Speech, being a spatializing medium only for social communication, is, for Dorothy Richardson and Bergson, an
impediment to the smooth flow of consciousness. In silence[37]
alone the psychic waters gather volume and begin to speed
on:

"There would not be any talk . . . silently the room filled
and overflowed. Turning at last from her window, Miriam
glanced at her sisters and let her thoughts drop into the
flowing tide."[38]

The image of the room filling and overflowing occurs
sometimes in the course of this narrative. In *Deadlock* she
seems to justify her label "fountain of consciousness":

"Freely watching the peaceful face in the mirror, she
washed with an intense sense of sheltering companionship. Far
in behind the peaceful face serene thoughts moved, not to and
fro, but outward and forward from some sure centre".[39]

She parts company with Bergson whenever she tries to
locate the source of psychic states at "some sure centre", for
according to him the centre itself is involved in a process of
ceaseless change.

*　　*　　*　　*　　*　　*

One of the fundamental problems confronting Dorothy Richardson as a novelist is how to realize *"les données immédiates de la conscience"*, seize this living reality before it deadens into a stereotyped image. Whereas a metaphysician, according to Bergson, can achieve this by immersing himself in the living flow of things, an artist must perforce represent this through a symbolical medium. The problem before the stream of consciousness novelist, therefore, is how to shorten this gap between *l'impression spontanée* and artistic representation. Proust expounds a similar theory through Elstir, the painter, whose intention is to express reality through naked sense perceptions in their original sequence before the meddling intellect has remoulded them into conventional patterns. It is this theory of Elstir's that Proust further elaborates in terms of the novelist's art in his concluding volume *Time Regained*, although he fails to carry it out in actual practice. Bergson states the same problem even more directly: the human mind always predisposed to perceiving with a view to action, is naturally confused when faced with a new order of perceptions unarranged by the intellect. But is the new order of perceptions, then, a distortion of reality? Is it not rather the only form of reality that an artist should try to represent?

Dorothy Richardson is acutely aware of this problem. Her intention as a novelist is to represent this unarranged order of sensory impressions. One of the devices employed by her to capture the original impulse, the nascent order of perceptions is the epistolary technique. In this respect she recalls to one's mind the similar efforts, though on a much more restricted canvas, of Samuel Richardson. This eighteenth-century analyst of the mind also explains, in his preface to *Clarissa Harlowe*, how his object is to transmit the undefiled original impulse. [40] Although his letters are not impressionistic like Dorothy Richardson's, he does attempt to represent thoughts in their nascent flow. This may be seen from the following extract from *Sir Charles Grandison*:

"Search everywhere—But you will, no doubt!—Suspect everybody—This Lady Betty Williams—Such a plot must have a woman in it. Was she not Sir Hargrave's friend?—This Sir Hargrave—Greville it would not be . . . But no more . . . forgive this distracted letter. I know not what I have written."[41]

These mental digressions are represented through such devices as parentheses, asides, post-scripts and interjectory statements, etc. Miriam Henderson is an enthusiastic correspondent, and one of her daily interests is to wait eagerly for "letters on the hall table"—letters from Hypo, Eve, Harriett, Alma, Amabel, Michael and others. But the letters she writes to others are not normal links of communication, because they are invariably given in their original form and are free from the inhibiting influence of the people addressed. For instance, the long letter in *The Tunnel*[42] beginning with "dear Eve, Shakespeare is a sound . . .", is torn up in the end because soon after Miriam finds it difficult to "recapture the impulse with which she had sat down". Other letters are so full of extraneous comments that the reader must always make an effort to edit the contents and sift for himself as to what was intended to be actually dispatched and what was mere personal musings. Here is a letter from her friend Alma Wilson rendered together with Miriam's immediate reactions:

"You dear old thing! . . . fell out of the sky this morning . . . to fill pages with 'you dear old thing!' . . . see you *at once*! *Immediately*! . . . come up to town and meet you . . . some sequestered tea-shop . . . our ancient heads together . . . tell you all that has happened to me since those days . . . next Thursday . . . let you know how really rejoiced I am . . . break the very elderly fact that I am married . . . but that makes no difference . . . 'all I have had the temerity to do . . .' What did that mean?"[43]

The significance of *l'impression spontanée*, which forms an important aspect of Bergson's philosophy, is duly recognized by both Dorothy Richardson and Proust. Both emphasize the aesthetic principle of registering the inner evolution of each impression and not representing, like the traditional novelist, its external marks only. This basic impulse behind the stream of consciousness technique is very forcefully expressed by Dorothy Richardson in one of Miriam's letters to Eve:

"She spent the evening writing to Eve, asking her if she remembered sea scenes at Weymouth and Brighton, pushing on and on weighed down by a sense of *the urgency of finding out whether,* to Eve, *the registration of impressions was a thing that she must either do or lose hold of something essential.* She felt that Eve would somehow admire her own stormy emphasis but would not really understand how much it meant to her."[44]

* * * * * *

As suggested earlier, *Pilgrimage* is more a journey through *la durée* than through space. It is in her durational presentation of personality that she resembles Bergson. For instance, Miriam's two-mile journey from London to Newlands, where she is to be governess to Mrs. Corrie's children, is, in fact, a drive through time, in passive contemplation of things past and in anticipation of new experiences:

"The journey was a long solitary adventure; endless; shielded from thoughts of the new life ahead . . . She could recall only the hours she had spent shivering apathetically over small fires . . . then the moment of accepting the new post . . . Spring—a sudden pang of tender green seen in suburban roadways in April, one day in the Easter holidays, bringing back the forgotten summer and showing you the whole picture of summer and autumn . . . Two years ago, when she had first gone out into the world, it had been March . . . the night journey from Barnes to London, and on down to Harwich . . . the moments passed, carrying her rapidly on."[45]

Miriam's journey from London to Newlands reminds one of Marcel's drive to the Prince de Guermantes',[46] except that whereas in her mind the past flows along the stream of associated memories of springs gone by, in Marcel's mind the familiar streets of the Champs-Élysées evoke a vision of the associated past and time elapsed.

In *Pilgrimage* Dorothy Richardson, like Proust, is concerned with the problem of finding a clue to *le temps perdu*, and although she does not evolve any explicit theory of time, she finds, none the less, the secret of all art in passive remembrance of things past. Like Proust again, it is one of her tasks to "find out exactly", as Miriam reflects during a music concert, *"what kind of experience it is that returns of itself, effortlessly"*,[47] for in such a revival alone, would time provide a key to the reality of aesthetic experience. "These strange unconsciously noticed things", she again muses in the course of her daily routine at the Wimpole Street office, "living on in one, coming together at the right moment, part of a *reality*".[48]

This durational medium in which the mind shuttles backward and forward, recalling past experiences in the already fading glow of the present moment, is nothing else than *la durée*. It is, in Bergson's words, "the continuous life of a memory which prolongs the past into the present, the present either containing within it in a distinct form the ceaselessly growing image of the past, or, more probably, showing by its continual change of quality the heavier and still heavier load we drag behind us as we grow older."[49] This load of the past, growing "heavier and heavier" with the passage of years, is the central theme of *Pilgrimage*. Such an experience of life obviously cannot be represented by such arbitrary symbols as hours, months and years, hence (to quote Dorothy Richardson), "the inadequacy of the clock as a time-measurer."

Unlike James Joyce and Virginia Woolf, Dorothy Richardson has not conducted any experiments with time. She does not choose a day as in *Mrs. Dalloway*, nor its cross-section as in *Ulysses*; nor again does she treat a space of about three hundred years as in *Orlando*, nor all time as in

Finnegans Wake. She presents in *Pilgrimage* only a normal span of Miriam's adolescence and youth from the age of seventeen to thirty-one. She further indicates such time-intervals as six months at Hanover, fifteen months at Pernes's Junior school, only to imply that such time-divisions are quite inadequate since they try to impose an arbitrary pattern on the dynamic evolution of personality through *la durée.*

After her return from Newlands, as Miriam takes up her lodgings with Mrs. Bailey at Tansley Street, St. Pancras clock, like Big Ben in *Mrs. Dalloway*, becomes a regular intruder into her inner consciousness. This obtrusive nature of external time is suggested in a symbolical incident in which Miriam, deeply engrossed in her song, is rudely accosted by a stranger.

"The figure of a man in an overcoat and a bowler hat loomed towards her on the narrow pathway and stopped. The man raised his hat, and his face showed smiling, with the moonlight on it. Miriam had a moment's fear; but the man's attitude was deprecating and there was her song . . . fierce anger at the recurrence of this kind of occurrence seized her. She wanted him out of the way and wanted him to know how angry she was at the interruption."

As she snaps at him, the stranger steps quickly into the gutter and walks away across the road. "St. Pancras church chimed the quarter. Miriam marched angrily forward with shaking limbs"[50] and her consciousness, related only to inner duration ("her song"), again begins to flow regardless of the stranger's interruption and the chiming of St. Pancras.

Time, according to Dorothy Richardson, is a stream and therefore cannot be divided into such pure tenses as the past, present and future. The present moment, which may outwardly appear to have an independent identity of its own, is in truth the shadow of the past projecting itself into the future. This fluid nature of time dawns within her consciousness whenever Miriam descends into the soul's depths in silence and solitude. Walking back home one evening, she suddenly realizes, "with a shock of surprise . . . *how powerfully the future flows into the present and how, on entering an experience, one is already beyond it,* so that most occasions are imperfect because no one is really quite within them, save before and afterwards; and then only at the price of solitude."[51] (*Clear Horizon*)

How close is the intimacy between Dorothy Richardson and Bergson with regard to their conception of time may be seen from an extract from *Matter and Memory*. "The essence of time", says Bergson, "is that it goes by . . . what I call 'my present' has one foot in my past and another in my future. In my past, first, because 'the moment in which I am speaking is already far from me'; in my future, next, because this moment is impending over the future . . ."[52]

Dorothy Richardson's method bears further resemblance to Bergson's presentation of the present moment of experience in its capacity to reveal both past and future. According to him, the associationists present a completely false picture of our mental processes in treating ideas as simple elements, atomic entities, capable of lending themselves to a mechanical mixture. Bergson does not dispute the contention of the associationists that every idea has a relation of similarity or contiguity with the previous mental state. His criticism, however, is based on the objection that such an explanation "throws no light on the mechanism of association; nor, does it really tell us anything at all."[53] The fault with the associationist theory is that it tries to over-intellectualize ideas. The correct explanation, according to Bergson, lies in "the undivided unity of perception."[54] Similarity or contiguity becomes meaningless unless it is itself accounted for. The truth is "that our entire personality, with the totality of our re- collections, is present, undivided within our actual perception. Then, if this perception evokes in turn different memories, it is not by a mechanical adjunction of more and more numerous elements which, while it remains itself unmoved, it attracts around it, but rather by an expansion of the entire consciousness which, spreading out over a larger area, discovers the fuller detail of its wealth."[55]

This expansion of the present moment of experience to its larger dimensions, in an attempt to discover "the fuller detail of its wealth", is precisely what Dorothy Richardson implies by "the inner expansibility of space",[56] or the possibility of achieving "a certain expansion of the consciousness at certain moments".[57]

The working of Miriam Henderson's associative consciousness cannot be analysed in terms of "similarity or contiguity" as its true explanation lies in this inner expansion. In the course of a first meeting with Michael Shatov who delivers a long monologue on Russia, Miriam's mind experiences "the irrevocable expansion of her consciousness"[58] over a vast space of mental landscape. To aesthetic minds of great sensibility alone is given the capacity to experience such moments of expansion at more frequent intervals and with greater perspicacity. No wonder it is with a feeling of great self-complacence that Miriam compares herself with Mr. Orly. "One *moment* of my consciousness", she tells Michael, "is wider and deeper than his has been in the whole of his life."[59]

The landscape over which the present expands is nothing else than *la durée*—a heterogeneous medium in which our states of consciousness are perpetually interpenetrating qualitatively.

*   *   *   *   *   *

Dorothy Richardson, like Bergson, treats memory as a "spiritual" phenomenon and its "offerings" as revelations of a reality which normally remains buried under the thick layers of habit and action. *Mémoire* is essentially *l'essence fondamentale* of *Pilgrimage*; the primary intention of the author is to employ it in recreating an entire past.

The past is a bottomless container of all experience which sends out in brief flashes its messages, particularly in moments of heightened perception, although its conditioning of the present moment is ceaseless. In *Revolving Lights* Dorothy Richardson affirms this Bergsonian belief in the perpetual existence of past life: "all the past was with her (Miriam) unobstructed; not recalled, but present, so that she could move into any part and be there as before."[60] Our constant preoccupation with the present makes this eternal link with the past weak and ineffective, but the past "was always there", reflects Miriam, "impossible, when one looked back . . . It made no break in the new life. The new life flowed through it, sunlit. It was a flight down strange vistas . . . the door of retreat always open . . ."[61]

In *Clear Horizon*, Dorothy Richardson compares this ineffaceable past to a "hiding place" whence emerge memories like leaping phantoms to waylay the unwary traveller on life's highway. "The incident had sprung forth unsummoned from its hiding place in the past where all these years it had awaited the niche prepared for it . . ."[62] And thus we carry the dead weight of our memories although "we prefer to imagine ourselves unencumbered". Those who are artists realize the significance of these memories as mysterious links with the reality of aesthetic experience. This explains why the urge to remember is persistent and paramount in Miriam's consciousness. "Nothing was so strong as the desire that everything would stop for a moment, and allow her to remember."[63] Miriam's consciousness seldom flows unalloyed with recollections, her self is ceaselessly recreating itself through contemplation of the past. "There is within oneself something", she says in *Clear Horizon*, "that ceaselessly contemplates 'forgotten' things . . ."[64] Dorothy Richardson's place is, therefore, with the other Bergsonian rememberers of the past, seekers after *le temps perdu*.

The creative mind that perpetually contemplates past experiences is obviously passive and detached from immediate action, but is not without sufficient awareness of the process of creation. It may here be noted how Bergson has been mis-interpreted by certain literary critics. One school of criticism asserts that in identifying life with action, Bergson has clearly assigned a derogatory place to *mémoire involontaire*. L. A. Bisson, in an article entitled "Proust, Bergson and George Eliot", argues from this premise to infer that Bergson does not recognize involuntary memory.[65]

On the other hand H. B. Parkes, in an article in *Scrutiny* entitled "The Tendencies of Bergsonism", presents Bergson's theory of memory as a plea for complete withdrawal from activity. "We are most spiritual", comments Parkes, "when we are least involved in action. Bergsonism may also, there-fore, be used to justify a neuropathic withdrawal from life." He then proceeds to substantiate his arguments by citing the example of Proust, Bergson's "most distinguished disciple" and observes, "if this may seem fanciful, one need only remark that precisely this conclusion was drawn by . . . Marcel Proust . . . To relive the past in memory was to live in the spirit. In Proust's novel the Bergsonian philosophy is transmuted into great art . . . Bergsonism of this kind is the philosophy of an invalid, separated from actuality, who occupies himself with reverie and dream."[66] Parkes would perhaps apply the same criticism to the work of Dorothy Richardson and cite it as yet another example of Bergsonian withdrawal from life and activity.

Yet it will be seen that both these extreme views presented by Bisson and Parkes show a lack of understanding of Bergson's distinction between voluntary and involuntary memory. When, for instance, Bergson says that the past images survive with a view to "utility",[67] he uses this word in reference only to *l'homme d'action*, the average man who lives mostly in the present. This does not imply, as Bisson wrongly suggests, that voluntary memory, deliberately selecting past images with a view to action, is the only authentic form of memory. Such a view of memory could be applicable only to the normal psychic life which is always preoccupied with the problems of immediate present and future, of action and necessity. Bergson says, "to live only in the present . . . is the mark of the lower animals."[68] He then proceeds to say that "to call up the past in the form of an image, we must be able to withdraw ourselves from the action of the moment, we must have the power to value the useless, we must have the will to dream. Man alone is capable of such an effort."[69] In contrast with this aesthetic view of experience, normal life "implies the acceptance only of the *utilitarian* side of things in order to respond to them by appropriate reactions: all other impressions must be dimmed or else reach us vague and blurred . . . From time to time, however, in a fit of absentmindedness, nature raises up souls that are more detached from life"—these are the souls of artists. ". . . did the soul no longer cleave to action", observes Bergson in *Laughter,* "by any of its perceptions, it would be the soul of an artist such as the world has never yet seen."[70] In these words Bergson explains how action and, therefore, its offspring voluntary memory, are essentially of a lower order than *mémoire involontaire* which, detached from immediate necessity, stores up images without any ulterior purpose.

It may be pointed out that a state of pure dream, of extreme absentmindedness and complete withdrawal from phenomena, as implied by Parkes, is not a congenial frame of mind for any artistic creation. The "dream" state necessary for any creative process is described by Bergson in his essay on "Dreams". Basing his observations on Stevenson's experience of literary creation, he says, ". . . when mind is creating, when it is giving the effort which the composition of a work of art . . . requires, it is not actually asleep. I mean that the part of the mind which is working is not the same as that which is dreaming: the working part is pursuing its task in the subconscious."[71] This "working" part is, therefore, an abstraction from the dreaming self, thus diluting its dreaminess and making possible the process of literary creation.

The work of Dorothy Richardson illustrates this "dreamy" state of mind which is an important prerequisite of all literary composition. Miriam Henderson is, in many respects, an exact replica of her creator.[72] It will, therefore, be interesting to analyse "dreaminess" as an important aspect of her consciousness. For instance, her thought processes are quickened and the stream of her thought begins to flow more smoothly when her mind falls into a relaxed state of reverie and starts "contemplating" phenomena. Then images from the past issue out of "their hiding-place" and take possession of her soul. This typical state of Miriam's consciousness is repeatedly stressed as a semi-conscious awareness of environment, because in such moments the self turns inwards upon its past and begins to dwell in the twilight zone of past-present. To give only a few examples of this "dreamy" state of mind:

"When Miriam woke the next morning she lay still with closed eyes. She had dreamt that she had been standing in a room in the German school . . ."[73] (*Pointed Roofs*)

". . . pushing the letter under the pillow and kneeling up to turn out the gas. When she lay down again her mind was rushing on by itself . . ."[74] (*Backwater*)

"When she turned out the gas . . . lay down . . . the air about her head . . . was full of her untrammelled thoughts."[75] (*The Tunnel*)

It is obvious that it is only in a passive state of mind that Miriam finds it possible to establish close contact with her past and discover in the pattern of her experience a unifying thread.

These retrospective musings serve another purpose in *Pilgrimage*. It is through Miriam's stream of consciousness that many links in the narrative are supplied. For instance, towards the end of the second chapter of *Pointed Roofs*, we collect some useful information about her parents and early environments.

"She thought sleepily of her Wesleyan grandparents . . . the shop at Babington, her father's discontent, his solitary

fishing and reading, his discovery of music . . . marriage . .
the birth of Sarah, and then Eve . . . and after five years her
own disappointing birth as the third girl . . . her mother's
illness, money troubles . . ."[76]

Here in a single paragraph is material enough for a number
of chapters full of drama and suspense, whereas for Dorothy
Richardson these narrative details form only capricious links
with the past, thrown up by the "spontaneous offerings of
memory".

Although Dorothy Richardson is aware of the importance
of memory to an artist, and her treatment of it is fairly
comprehensive, she does not suggest any formal distinction
between voluntary and involuntary memory. She moves
freely from one to the other implying that in the actual
process of remembering both forms are inextricably blended.
In this respect she differs from both Bergson and Proust. A
taste or an odour may evoke *involuntarily* a certain past
experience but as the stream of thought begins to flow along a
particular channel, it often comes at a later stage under the
influence of a directive force whose interests are to unfold
that experience in all its relevant and significant details. In
other words, an "unsummoned" remembrance is likely to be
succeeded by a "summoned" recollection to help, as it were,
the original impulse in discovering the fuller details of its
wealth. This is implied in a very suggestive passage in *Backwater*
where Miriam, leaving behind Eve and Miss Stringer, strays
alone over the Brighton rocks and finds her mind "sliding out"
untethered along an involuntary stream of memories of her
childhood at Dawlish:

"At the end of half an hour's thoughtless wandering over
the weed-grown rocks, she found herself sitting on a little
patch of dry silt . . . watching the gentle rippling of the
retreating waves over the weedy lower levels. She seemed
long to have been listening and watching, her mind was full
of things she felt she would never forget . . . Her mind slid

out making a strange half-familiar compact with all these things . . . She had always known them, she reflected, remembering with a quick pang a long, unpermitted wandering over the cliff edge beyond Dawlish, the sun shining on pinkish sandy scrub, the expression on the bushes . . . She must have been about six years old."[77]

This involuntary vision of the past, laden with all such little details as "the sun shining on pinkish sandy scrub" and "the expression of the bushes," lying buried under the routine of life, upsurges suddenly in a moment of passive receptivity. But soon after, this involuntary memory tries to seek the aid of deliberate memory in order to complete the pattern of the recalled experience, thus involving itself in a conscious effort "in the search for a particular image".[78] A later part of the same passage demonstrates this inevitable blending in all recollections of both forms of memory:

"*She tried to remember* when the strange independent joy had begun, and thought she *could trace it back* to a morning in the garden at Babington, the first thing she could remember, when she had found herself toddling alone along the garden path between beds of flowers almost on a level with her head and blazing in the sunlight."[79]

Although these sensations, preserved in their original detail, emerge from "pure memory" they later on assume the form of "acquired recollections" to complete the antecedents of a vision evoked involuntarily. These memories, voluntary or involuntary, are, according to Dorothy Richardson, "more real than anything else in the world".[80]

How does one form of memory merge into another is a problem that has been left untouched by Bergson and Proust, because in their attempt to distinguish between the two forms of memory they do not foresee the possibility in art of their constant intermingling. The truth seems to be that a memory emerging into consciousness involuntarily often needs the help of deliberate memory to complete its pattern. In other words, a past experience evoked involuntarily in the form of a nebulous mass of images must needs crystallize itself round a central thread to become distinct and recognizable. On the other hand, it would be equally true to say that an image re-called voluntarily is likely to spread itself over a wider canvas and ultimately lose itself in a mass of "unsummoned images".

Like Proust, Dorothy Richardson believes in the power of an object, odour, or taste to recall a past experience. Miriam's "Liberty brooch", Michael's botany scissors, and the "moss-green ewer" are, therefore, invested with a life all their own. They form mysterious links with the entire range of her past experience. A human face may evoke such a recollection, but "individual objects", observes Miriam, "hold the power of moving one deeply and immediately and always in the same way". On the other hand, "people move one variously and intermittently and, in direct confrontation, there is nearly always a barrier. In things, even in perfectly 'ordinary and commonplace' things, life is embodied. The sudden sight of a sun-faded garment can arouse from where they lie stored in oneself, sleeping memories, the lovely essences of a summer holiday, free from all that at the moment seemed to come between oneself and the possibility of passionate apprehension. *After an interval, only after an interval*—showing that there is within oneself something that ceaselessly contemplates 'forgotten' things—a fragment of stone, even a photograph, has the power of making one enter a kingdom one hardly knew one possessed. Whose riches increase, even though they are inanimate."[81]

This is a typical Proustian statement[82] of the aesthetic significance of involuntary memories. Not at the moment of perceiving a phenomenon, but only "after an interval", allow-ing memory sufficient time to absorb and later re-present it in fuller perspective, can one realize its true reality. Thus far Dorothy Richardson follows Bergson closely but she parts company with him when she asserts that objects move us "always in the same way", whereas, according to Bergson, the perceiving self itself, a part of the ceaseless flux, is perpetually growing in duration and undergoing a constant change of point of view.

* * * * * *

It is necessary to point out at this stage that although Dorothy Richardson's *Pilgrimage* has a certain historical importance in the development of the English novel, it pales into insignificance when compared with the novels of Virginia Woolf or James Joyce. Devoid of any dramatic interest, symbolic meaning òr skilful patterning, *Pilgrimage* remains at best only a literal and rather uninteresting record of Miriam's stream of consciousness. Dorothy Richardson contents herself with choosing brief intervals of Miriam's experience, and within these periods there is hardly any selection. Unlike Virginia Woolf or James Joyce, she does not attempt to reconcile Miriam's stream of thought with any design or pattern. No rhythmic tones, contrasts of mood or situation, relieve the monotony of her narrative which seems to continue in its primordial flow. She appears to be unaware of the imperative need to superimpose some kind of aesthetic design on the indeterminate flow of Miriam's stream of sensory impressions.

Both Virginia Woolf and James Joyce achieve this in different ways: the former by investing character and scene with symbolic meaning, and the latter by an extremely subtle interweaving of themes and patterns, and also by modelling *Ulysses* on the *Odyssey* parallel. Their novels, in spite of a seemingly unregulated fluidity, invariably represent an architectonic schematization of experience. Even as theorists of fiction, they are both acutely aware of the necessity to represent *la durée* in an intelligible and communicable form, for a blind adherence to the Bergsonian flux could never be aesthetically satisfying.

In *A Writer's Diary*, Virginia Woolf grapples with the problem of reconciling flux with form. Although she admits that "the irregular fire must be there",[83] "yet everything must have relevance".[84] Her task as a novelist is "to saturate every atom . . . to eliminate all waste, deadness, superfluity".[85] Why include anything, she further adds, that lacks poetic intensity? "Is that not my grudge against novelists? that they select nothing? . . ."—she might have been referring to Dorothy Richardson—"I want to put practically everything in: *yet to saturate*."[86]

As a novelist, she claims to be a "formalist", always preoccupied with problems of "vision and design".[87] ". . . I think writing must be formal", she writes in her diary, "the art must be respected . . . for if one lets the mind run loose it becomes egoistic . . ."[88] This is precisely where she differs from Dorothy Richardson—in patterning her material instinctively. Her preoccupations with form and design are evident from her notes on the genesis and development of the theme of *The Waves*. She seems to be constantly worried over the task of making her novel acquire "coherence and effect". "I am not sure of the effect artistically; because the proportions may need the intervention of the waves finally so as to make a conclusion."[89]

There is no attempt to create any artistic effects in *Pilgrimage*, nor does Dorothy Richardson ever seem to "conclude" her narrative. As suggested earlier, her novels are less successful because she goes on with the flux indefinitely till she is too tired to continue any further. If form is to be defined in Virginia Woolf's words as "the sense that one thing follows another rightly",[90] then it may be remarked that there is no form in *Pilgrimage*. Dorothy Richardson thus remains the least successful of all the stream of consciousness novelists.

CHAPTER **4**

Virginia Woolf

IT WOULD BE USELESS TO CONTINUE ANY
further the controversy as to whether or not Virginia Woolf
was influenced by Bergson to whose theories of flux and
intuition her work seems to bear a very close resemblance.
It is almost certain that she had never read Bergson in the
original, nor was she influenced by his philosophy in her style
and presentation of *la durée* and memory.[1] The truth seems
to be that her work provides yet another example of parallelism
between the stream of consciousness technique and the
Bergsonian flux.

Before inquiring into this parallelism, it may be interesting
to recapitulate the theories of those critics who have always
insisted upon a direct relationship between Virginia Woolf
and Bergson, if only to show how they have often been led
to base their arguments on rather inconclusive evidence.[2] For
instance, it is assumed that Virginia Woolf must have read her
sister-in-law's brilliant exposition of Bergsonism which was
published in 1922 under the title *The Misuse of Mind—A Study
of Bergson's Attack on Intellectualism*. To quote Floris Delattre:

"En s'appuyant surtout sur les définitions de la perception,
de la matière et de la mémoire, Mrs. Karin Stephen décrit

64

dans le détail la conception bergsonienne de la réalité, conception de tous points originale, affirme-t-elle, et 'qui ne sera intelligible que si nous sommes désireux et capables d'effectuer un profond changement dans notre attitude'. [3] Il est vraisemblable que Virginia Woolf n'a point tout à fait ignoré l'ouvrage de sa belle-soeur, travail que Bergson lui-même a déclaré 'intéressant au plus haut point' . . ."[4]

Proust has been presented as another link between Virginia Woolf and Bergson.[5] It is suggested that Virginia Woolf's brother-in-law, Clive Bell, who published his little book on Proust in 1928, was largely responsible for introducing the French philosopher to the literary and artistic circles in which Virginia Woolf moved.[6] Extracts from this book are sometimes ingeniously related to similar statements in the work of Virginia Woolf to show how she had come to acquire Bergson's ideas through Clive Bell's commentary on Proust:

"Proust saw human beings as clouds of midges floating in time, ever changing, ever becoming, never still. Bergson was his master and—as may or may not care to know—his relation by marriage: also a student of Proust might do worse than read a little Bergson . . . to realize that the form of the novel is a shape in time . . ."[7]

It might as well be added that T. S. Eliot, another sympathizer of the Bloomsbury circle and a close literary associate of Virginia Woolf,[8] was a Bergsonian in the second decade of this century and still continues to show signs of early "saturation" with *durée réelle*.[9]

Roger Fry and Desmond MacCarthy, two other members of the Bloomsbury group, one might continue arguing, were introduced to Bergsonism through its partial manifestation in the contemporary post-impressionistic painting, which realized for purposes of art the importance of the immediacy of experience rendered in a fluid medium. In a dedicatory letter to Roger Fry, in his translation of Jules Romains' Bergsonian novel *The Death of a Nobody*, Desmond MacCarthy wrote: ". . . because you believe that something analogous to Post-impressionism is possible and desirable in literature, because in M. Jules Romains' work there is a flavour of it, we dedicate this translation to you."[10] And he visualized in this book the opening of "a path in a direction towards which some writers are feeling their way. I can conceive M. Jules Romains having an influence in this country upon a few who may influence others."[11]

This does not imply that Desmond MacCarthy or Roger Fry subscribed to Bergson's philosophy. They were, however, fully aware of the new possibilities in literature suggested by this philosophy of reality as an eternal process of flux and change. It would hardly serve any purpose to pursue this line of reasoning further to conclude that Virginia Woolf was acquainted with Bergsonism through its presentation in Jules Romains's novel which was enthusiastically appreciated by her close literary associates.

There are other critics who relate Virginia Woolf's technique as a novelist to the symbolist modes of expression, and then suggest that symbolism was only another variation of Bergsonism.[12] But we have already referred to the fallacy of treating Bergsonism and symbolism as mutually influencing each other, since both these movements were almost simultaneous manifestations of the new awareness of experience as continuity.

Edmund Wilson brings out this resemblance between the metaphysics implicit in Bergsonism and Symbolism. Just as Symbolism represented a new way of rendering reality free from traditional conceptualization, so was Bergsonism a plea for a free intuitive process of creative evolution against the more mechanistic theories of nineteenth-century materialism. While defining the nature of language as employed by the symbolists, Wilson observes that "such a language must make use of symbols: what is so special, so fleeting and so vague cannot be conveyed by direct statement or description, but only by a succession of words, of images, which will serve to suggest it to the reader."[13] Such a creative effort is also the ideal of Bergsonian aesthetic which invalidates any attempt to bind mobile reality within a rigid framework. In *The Waves*, a typical symbolist novel, Virginia Woolf suggests in a fluid style the fleeting states of consciousness through a quick succession of images.

Since direct statement or description cannot represent reality in all its "sinuosities",[14] the symbolist employs the medium of "a complicated association of ideas represented by a medley of metaphors . . ."[15] This sums up very adequately both the form and content of a novel like *The Waves*, which presents successfully the Bergsonian view of personality as a process of dynamic evolution. Between the symbolist's notion of reality as a qualitative organization of different units and Bergson's concept of *durée réelle* there is a marked resemblance. But whereas it may thus be possible to explain Virginia Woolf's art as a novelist in terms of symbolism, it would be rather far-fetched and even misleading to press this parallelism into establishing her indirect relationship with Bergson.

In the course of this brief résumé, we have tried to suggest how none of these theories of direct or indirect relationship yields any conclusive evidence. Any attempt to establish Virginia Woolf's relationship with Bergson through Mrs. Karin Stephen, Proust, T. S. Eliot, the Bloomsburies, the post-impressionists or the symbolists would hardly offer any fruitful results. It may be repeated here that she had never read Bergson, nor would she have admitted his indirect influence on her work. This view is also corroborated by both Leonard Woolf and Clive Bell. "I don't think that Virginia Woolf ever read a word by Bergson or Karin Stephen's book, *The Misuse of Mind*", writes Leonard Woolf,[16] and so does Clive Bell affirm, "I doubt whether Virginia Woolf ever opened a book by Bergson."[17]

Virginia Woolf was an exceptionally individualistic writer who had discovered her bearings at an early stage and formulated her own theories regarding the nature of reality and experience. The true explanation of the Bergsonian character of her novels lies in her being a manifestation, like many other contemporary novelists, of the *Zeitgeist*. Quite independently of any "influences", she was evolving a literary and philosophical outlook which has tempted many critics, not unsurprisingly, into assuming a direct relationship. In reality, if she strikes one as a typical Bergsonian novelist, it is because of the marked *parallelism* between her use of the stream of consciousness method and the durational flux.

*　*　*　*　*　*

"And all our intuitions mock
The formal logic of the clock."
(W. H. Auden: *New Year Letter*)

Of all the stream of consciousness novelists, Virginia Woolf alone seems to have presented a consistent and comprehensive treatment of time. Time with her is almost a mode of perception, a filter which distils all phenomena before they are apprehended in their true significance and relationship. Her characters, like those of Proust, are "monsters occupying a place in Time infinitely more important than the restricted one reserved for them in space".[18] Her protest against the Edwardian novel was, in fact, a revolt against the tyranny of chronological time that is "matter" in favour of *la durée* that is "spirit". This also explains why she considers Joyce and other contemporary novelists of the time-school to be "spiritualists" as against the "materialism" of Galsworthy, Bennett and Wells. All her literary experiments as a novelist can be explained in terms of Bergson's *la durée*. In fact, it is possible to trace her development from the point of view of her progressive awareness of the various aspects of psychological time.

Time has always been one of the most baffling problems for the novelist. It is, says Henry James, "that side of the novelist's effort—the side of most difficulty and thereby of most dignity—which consists in giving the sense of duration, of the lapse and accumulation of time. This is altogether to my view the stiffest problem that the artist in fiction has to tackle."[19] It was towards this problem that Virginia Woolf addressed her main efforts as a novelist. Her various literary experiments are, in fact, directed towards finding a suitable medium which could render most appropriately this elusive "sense of duration".

However, before interpreting her work in terms of Bergson's durational flux, it may be interesting to compare her with Sterne who had conducted similar experiments with time and evolved a highly fluid and indeterminate type of narrative. In her essay on "The Sentimental Journey", Virginia Woolf presents him as "the forerunner of the moderns". "No writing", she says, "seems to flow more exactly into the very folds and creases of the individual mind, to express its changing moods, to answer its slightest whim and impulse . . . *the utmost fluidity exists.*"[20]

Sterne is undoubtedly the first time-novelist who had, as early as 1760, anticipated some of the fictional experiments of James Joyce, Virginia Woolf and Dorothy Richardson. He was the first to revolt against the rigours of chronological sequence of time. This is how the narrator in *Tristram Shandy* presents the qualitative aspect of time which can never be assessed in terms of such statistical terms as minutes, hours, months and years. This theme forms the subject of a discussion between Mr. Shandy and Uncle Toby:

". . . my father . . . was pre-determined in his mind to give my Uncle Toby a clear account of the matter by a metaphysical dissertation upon the subject of duration and its simple modes", and after these preliminary remarks Mr. Shandy proceeds to give a more elaborate description of "duration" and the succession of ideas after the manner of John Locke.[21] "*. . . in our computations of time, we are so used to minutes, hours, weeks, and months—and of clocks* (I wish there was not a clock in the kingdom) *to measure out their several portions to us . . .* Now, whether we observe it or no, continued my father, in every sound man's head there is *a regular succession of ideas* of one sort or other, which follow each other in train . . ."[22]

Although dressed in a humorous garb, this passage appropriately brings out the importance of inner duration to a psychological novelist whose primary intention should be faithfully to render the "regular succession of ideas". But Sterne's approach to duration being Lockean, he can conceive psychic phenomena only as discrete elements capable of being arranged in juxtaposition alongside of each other in a homogeneous medium which is nothing else than space. The metaphor employed by Mr. Shandy in describing Locke's theory of ideas is that of a *train*.[23] This conception of duration is obviously atomistic and retains under the guise of continuity the whole apparatus of numerical multiplicity. We are, therefore, still far from Bergson's concept of duration as a medium in which all psychic states permeate one another in a qualitative process, like notes in a musical phrase.[24]

To understand Virginia Woolf's treatment of *la durée* in her novels, it would be necessary to note the difference between Locke's spatial analysis of duration and Bergson's presentation of it as a qualitative process of creative evolution. It could, therefore, be remarked that just as Locke is the informing spirit behind *Tristram Shandy,* so might Bergson have been the philosophic inspiration behind Virginia Woolf's realization of *la durée.* Quite instinctively, she employs metaphors which unlike Sterne's, do not suggest a process of quantitative assemblage, but, like Bergson's, present duration as a ceaseless succession of qualitative changes.

Here is, for instance, her description of the chiming of Big Ben in *Mrs. Dalloway*:

"(The leaden circles dissolved in the air) . . . It is half-past eleven, she says, and the sound of St. Margaret's glides into the recesses of the heart and buries itself in ring after ring of sound, like something alive which wants to confide itself, to disperse itself, to be, with a tremor of delight, at rest—like Clarissa herself, thought Peter Walsh, coming downstairs . . ."[25]

In this passage Virginia Woolf apprehends the chiming of St. Margaret's only as a process of inner interpenetration, thus converting external clock time into a subjective living phenomenon.

Time being one of the most significant aspects of the work of Virginia Woolf, it should be possible to trace her development as a novelist in terms of her gradual swing from a traditional view of time to Bergson's *durée*.

Her two early novels, *The Voyage Out* (1915) and *Night and Day* (1919) are written in the traditional style and present personality in a chronological sequence of events arranged along a linear movement progressing towards a well-defined climax. Rachel Vinrace, initiated from adolescence into youth by an unexpected kiss from Richard Dalloway, sympathetically encouraged along the path of self-discovery by her aunt Helen Ambrose, finally realizes her true self in an all-absorbing emotional experience before death which comes as the last definitive stroke in this vast progressive, unilateral, temporal movement. The clock here assumes its traditional role and, except for announcing hours and suggesting conventional analogies, has no deeper significance.

Rachel Vinrace has been reading a novel: "The morning was hot, and the exercise of reading left her mind contracting and expanding like the mainspring of a clock. The sounds in the garden outside joined with the clock, and the small noises of midday, which one can ascribe to no definite cause . . ."[26]

Night and Day which followed four years later also continues the traditional method of presenting life in a chronological sequence. Katherine Hilbery, the grand-daughter of a famous poet, brought up in a sophisticated atmosphere, is provoked by Ralph Denham into recognizing other ways of living and thinking, till through a course of well-patterned vicissitudes smoothing their respective angularities, they join hands in marriage. The clock once again performs the docile function of announcing convenient hours of transition from one phase of consciousness to another. "The nine mellow strokes, by which she was now apprised of the hour, were a message from the great clock at Westminster itself. As the last of them died away, there was a firm knocking on her own door, and she rose and opened it."[27] It may here be noted that the clock does not break in upon an unprepared consciousness but strikes only at a convenient moment.

With *Jacob's Room* we enter into an entirely new phase of Virginia Woolf's career as a novelist. Published three years after *Night and Day*, during which interval she had experimented freely in her stories and sketches,[28] *Jacob's Room* marks an important development in her treatment of *la durée*. Although these stories and sketches (published under the title *Monday and Tuesday*) do not reveal any clear consciousness of duration, they are none the less instrumental in sharpening a sensibility which could later apprehend the subjective notion of time. In this novel we are made to feel the impotence of calendar time in its attempt to superimpose an arbitrary pattern on the continuity of inner experience. Even the external phenomena of life are here shown as flowing in a qualitative succession of their own, regardless of the clock-cut "spaces of complete immobility" which seem to separate "each of the movements". In a passage in *Jacob's Room* Virginia Woolf suggests Nature's massive indifference towards man-made clock divisions which can never cohere with her inner laws:

"Black shadows stood still over the silver moors. The furze bushes stood perfectly still. Neither did Mrs. Jarvis think of God. There was a church behind them, of course. The church clock struck ten. *Did the strokes reach the furze bush, or did the thorn tree hear them?*"[29]

And again, "The clock struck the quarter. The frail waves of sound broke among the stiff gorse and the hawthorn twigs *as the church clock divided them into quarters.*

Motionless and broad-backed the moors received the statement 'It is fifteen minutes past the hour', but made no answer, unless a bramble stirred . . . Their tongues join together in syllabling the sharp-cut words, *which for ever slice asunder time* and the broad-backed moors . . . But at midnight when no one speaks or gallops, and the thorn tree is perfectly still, it would be foolish to vex the moor with questions—what? and why?

The church clock, *however*, strikes twelve."[30]

The clock which, *however,* must strike is an unpleasant intruder into the inner continuity of man and nature. In fact, it is only a symbol of the present which, like "habit, action or body", is a material phenomenon, trying to effect, in an arbitrary manner, a breach in the otherwise continuous flow of *la durée*. "The essence of time is that it goes by", observes Bergson, "time already gone by is the past, and we call the present the instant in which it goes by."[31] But he adds that "there can be no question here of a mathematical instant", which it is the function of the clock to impress upon the mind with precision.

La durée, on the other hand, is the movement implicit in a rapid succession and interpenetration of the snapshots on a cinematograph film and cannot be identified with any single picture. *Jacob's Room,* like such a film, creates the illusion of Jacob's ceaseless becoming as he progresses through various experiences. The resultant impression of his personality on the reader's mind is harmonious and composite. To demonstrate, as it were, the arbitrariness of any particular moment singled out of the stream of *la durée*, Virginia Woolf selects in this novel the hour of five o'clock to show how such a tampering with *durée réelle* can only distort reality by presenting it in a static, spatialized form. This hour is intended to present a study in still life which is obviously a negation of the real dynamic experience. A few characters are shown frozen at a particular moment in the course of their life-movement. "The gilt clock at Verrey's was striking five . . . Jacob, *leaning forward*, drew a plan of the Parthenon in the dust in Hyde Park . . . read *a long flowing letter* which Sandra had written two days ago";[32] while she at the moment mused how Jacob was "like that man in Molière"; "even now poor Fanny Elmer *was dealing*, as she walked along the Strand, in her incompetent way with this very careless, indifferent, sublime manner he had of talking to railway guards or porters . . ."[33] Here "five strokes Big Ben intoned; Nelson received the salute. The wires of the Admiralty shivered with some faraway communication."[34] Timmy Durrant, at this moment, is seen in his "little room in the Admiralty, *going to consult* a Blue book . . . Miss Thomas, one of the typists, said to her friend that if the Cabinet *was going to sit* much longer she should miss her boy outside the Gaiety";[35] "'now I know that face'—said the Reverend Andrew Floyd, *coming out of* Carter's shop in Piccadilly, 'but who the dickens—'?"[36]

These characters, arrested in their life-flow, pose, as it were, for a moment before the camera, and break into movement again. The predominant tense, as referred to earlier, is not the preterite but the present continuous (e.g. "was dealing", "going to consult", etc.)

Mrs. Dalloway, published in 1925, marks another development in the evolution of Virginia Woolf's time-theme. Time broods over the entire narrative[37] and lends it a significance and purpose not always fully understood by all readers. Not only is the novel designed skilfully on a limited time-pattern, covering a single day in the life of Mrs. Dalloway, but it also shows a clearer understanding and presentation of *la durée* as the true essence of all aesthetic experience.

It is only on the surface level that Big Ben becomes the principle of plot-construction and lends coherence and intelligibility to the narrative lacking in *Jacob's Room*. It may be useful here to give a brief time-analysis of the plot. On a Wednesday morning in the middle of June, Mrs. Dalloway leaves her house to buy flowers; at eleven o'clock Peter Walsh pays his unexpected visit; at half-past eleven he is proceeding towards Trafalgar Square; at a quarter to twelve Septimus Smith recalls his deceased friend Evans; at twelve o'clock Mrs. Dalloway lays her dress on the bed; Septimus Smith and his wife, at this hour, enter Sir William Bradshaw's clinic; at half-past one Richard Dalloway attends Lady Bruton's lunch party in Brook Street; at three Septimus Smith commits suicide, later felt by Mrs. Dalloway as a personal disaster.

And yet, if we inquire into this time-scheme, we shall find that the operations of Big Ben in slicing the day into regular bits are limited only to external phenomena. The inner time, or *durée réelle*, yields to no such arbitrary divisions. The interval, for instance, between eleven o'clock and eleven-thirty is rich in intensity, unfolding the entire panorama of Mrs. Dalloway's past life at Bourton within the brief space of half an hour, whereas the much longer interval between three-thirty and six o'clock is comparatively not as important. In the mathematical time, "it is the t-th moment only that counts . . . What will flow on in the interval—that is to say, real time", says Bergson, "does not count, and cannot enter into the calculation."[38]

The central characters in this novel, particularly Septimus Smith and Clarissa Dalloway, live in *la durée* and not by clock time. Septimus Smith, who is engaged in writing an "ode to time", is a perfect embodiment of inner duration. He lives in a perpetual communion with the past through his recollections of his deceased friend Evans. Even his ultimate suicide seems to symbolize his complete defiance of the tyranny of clock time as represented by Sir William Bradshaw, who has taken upon himself the task of restoring the mental balance of his patients. He performs, in a sense, the same function as Big Ben, in attempting to regulate life's endless stream. In a remarkably suggestive passage, Virginia Woolf presents this aspect of Bradshaw's personality:

"Naked, defenceless, the exhausted, the friendless received the impress of Sir William's will. He swooped; he devoured. He shut people up . . . Rezia Warren Smith cried, walking down Harley Street, that she did not like that man.

"Shredding and slicing, dividing and subdividing, the clocks of Harley Street nibbled at the June day, counselled submission, upheld authority, and pointed out in chorus the supreme advantages of a sense of proportion, until the mound of time was so far diminished that a commercial clock, suspended above a shop in Oxford Street, announced, genially and fraternally, as if it were a pleasure to Messrs. Rigby and Lowndes to give the information gratis, that it was half-past one."[39]

Sir William Bradshaw and Dr. Holmes, "the repulsive brute, with the blood-red nostrils", in league with "the clocks of Harley Street", uphold the tyranny of external time over the inner stream of experience. Harley Street cannot, obviously, lead to that inner poise which is attainable only by letting the stream of consciousness flow on unimpeded. Reality, which is a process of becoming, is a dynamic continuity that cannot be sliced into proportionate bits and can be apprehended only through intuition.

To the Lighthouse, unlike *Mrs. Dalloway,* is limited to the space of ten years. In the three sections of the novel, we have three corresponding aspects of time represented symbolically. In the first section entitled, "The Window", covering about

two-thirds of the entire narrative, Virginia Woolf describes an
intense human experience in a mere cross-section of a
September evening from six o'clock to supper time. Therefore, whereas the clock covers only a couple of hours, it is
only through *la durée* that we are enabled to participate in
the inner experience of various characters. In Mrs. Ramsay
time becomes a symbol of inner expansion because she fills
it with love, hope and understanding; Mr. Ramsay's inordinate
egotism, on the other hand, contracts time; to James it is
synonymous with "tomorrow" and the promise of a visit to
the lighthouse; to Lily Briscoe time is a symbolic process of
the intaking of sensory impressions and memories. *La durée*, as
suggested in this novel, is a living organism. It is a qualitative
process and not an assemblage of discrete moments of
experience. ". . . how life", says Mrs. Ramsay, "from being
made up of little separate incidents which one lived one by
one, became curled and whole like a wave which bore one
up with it . . ."[40]

The second section, "Time Passes", brings into contrast
with the inner duration, the flow of external time—ten years.
Events, after Mrs. Ramsay's death, assume a different aspect
altogether. They are announced, rather unceremoniously,
within bracketed interpolations, beginning with Mrs. Ramsay's
death "the night before"; Prue Ramsay's marriage and death
a year later in child-birth; Andrew Ramsay's death by shell-
explosion; the publication of Carmichael's poems, etc. In the
march of these events and seasons, imponderable flow of
external time, "night and day, month and year ran shapelessly
together",[41] and thus time unrelated to Mrs. Ramsay becomes
a confused rout. *La durée*, Virginia Woolf indirectly suggests,
is not a medium of time-mensuration but almost a mode of
perception with its own aesthetic values. When the memory
of Mrs. Ramsay, after an interval of ten years, re-emerges in
the mind of Lily Briscoe (third section), the former again
begins to inspire her values in the minds of those who

remember, love and respect her. She becomes like Albertine "a mighty goddess of Time".[42]

The Ramsays' summer house is not an inanimate structure in three spatial dimensions, but like Proust's Combray church exists also in the fourth dimension—*la durée*. It becomes a durational link between the past and future, reassuming its significant role with the return of Lily Briscoe "one late evening in September". It symbolizes the point from which Lily Briscoe can "tunnel" back into the past in remembrance of Mrs. Ramsay, and Mr. Ramsay, together with James and Cam, can sail into the future on their expedition to the lighthouse. But these arbitrary segments of time, the past, present and future, merge into each other to form *durée réelle* when, on the one hand the party lands on the lighthouse and, on the other Lily Briscoe, in a moment of sudden revelation, realizes her vision. Lily Briscoe's painting seems to be designed on a durational pattern, since it derives its aesthetic validity from a qualitative interpenetration of the past, present and future.

"'He has landed' . . . 'It is finished.'

"Quickly, as if she were recalled by something over there, she turned to her canvas. There it was—her picture . . . she looked at her canvas; it was blurred. *With a sudden intensity*, as if she saw it clear for a second, *she drew a line there, in the centre. It was done*; it was finished. Yes, she thought, laying down her brush in extreme fatigue, I have had my vision."[43]

"He has landed . . . It is finished", and so is also finished the period of anxious travail in discovering the most appropriate blendings of colours, and in solving "the question . . . of some relation between those masses".[44] Then arrives the moment of illumination, and with a bold stroke Lily Briscoe draws a line in the centre. This definitive stroke symbolizes a sudden intuitive realization of the qualitative blending into each other of the mechanically separated segments of time. Not the present moment of experience, but only its recapitulation after an interval, can reveal its true essence by releasing it from the cramping influence of the immediate circumstances. Lily Briscoe could not have realized her vision earlier in the first section, because the personal presence of Mrs. Ramsay would have been an embarrassing distraction, disabling her from conceiving the picture in its true perspective. Ten years had to pass, the proposed expedition to the lighthouse had to materialize, before the final vision could dawn within her consciousness.[45]

Orlando is, in many respects, Virginia Woolf's *tour de force* in her treatment of *la durée*. It gathers up in a vast symphonic movement all the temporal themes presented earlier and all those which appear in her subsequent work. Here is, for instance, a suggestive passage which describes the lapse of time after Orlando's visit to Nick Green:

". . . he flung himself under his favourite oak tree . . . here he came then, day after day, week after week, month after month, year after year. He saw the beech trees turn golden and the young ferns unfurl . . . but probably the reader can imagine the passage which should follow and how . . . spring follows winter and autumn summer; how night succeeds day and day night . . . how things remain as they are for two or three hundred years or so, except for a little dust and a few cobwebs which *one old woman* can sweep up in half an hour; a conclusion which, one cannot help feeling, might have been reached more quickly by the simple statement that "Time Passed" (here the exact amount could be indicated in brackets) and nothing whatever happened."[46]

In this passage Virginia Woolf provides a key to the understanding of the middle section of *To the Lighthouse,* and the "one old woman" suggests very strongly Mrs. McNab who is employed by Mr. Ramsay in the intervening years to save the summer house from the wear and tear of Time's grinding wheel.

In the course of a subsequent passage, Virginia Woolf

explains the inadequacy of a conventional approach to the biographical theme. "But the biographer", she says, "whose interests are . . . highly restricted, must confine himself to one simple statement . . ."[47], a formal announcement with regard to the age a person has attained at a certain period of his life. The biographical theme as treated in *Jacob's Room*, however, shows personality as a process of becoming rather than as a mere accretion of experiences presented in a chronological sequence.

The elasticity of duration, Bergson's *durée*, is suggested in another passage in which Virginia Woolf shows how *its* ostensible "lengths" depend upon a subjective or objective apprehension of experience. If reflection or introspection prolongs *la durée*, "action or habit" contracts it. ". . . time when he is thinking becomes inordinately long; time when he is doing becomes inordinately short. Thus Orlando gave his orders and did the business of his vast estates in a flash; but directly he was alone on the mound under the oak tree, the seconds began to round and fill until it seemed as if they would never fall. *They filled themselves, moreover, with the strangest variety of objects.*"[48] This seems to recall Proust's similar presentation of *la durée*: "An hour", he says, "is not merely an hour, it is a vase filled with perfumes, with sounds, with objects, with climates."[49]

Reflection in a passive state of mind always opens, according to Bergson, the floodgates of past recollections which then "rushed into the falling second, swelled it a dozen times its natural size, coloured it a thousand tints, and filled it with all the odds and ends in the universe".[50] It is her realization of this durational elasticity that enables Virginia Woolf to indulge in all kinds of puckish gambols with chronological time in *Orlando*.[51]

The fundamental theme in the work of Virginia Woolf is the emphasis on the unbridgable gulf between *durée réelle* and the clock that "registers the hour in its usual cryptic way",[52] and whose only function is to intrude thunderingly into our mental processes. ("Like thunder, the stable clock struck four."[53]) Her basic aesthetic intention is to stress this discrepancy between the mechanical and psychological time. In a key passage in *Orlando*, she states this problem in very explicit terms:

"But Time, unfortunately, though it makes animals and vegetables bloom and fade with amazing punctuality, has no such simple effect upon the mind of man. The mind of man, moreover, works with equal strangeness upon the body of time. An hour, once it lodges in the queer element of the human spirit, may be stretched to fifty or a hundred times its clock length; on the other hand, an hour may be accurately represented on the timepiece of the mind by one second. *This extraordinary discrepancy between time on the clock and time in the mind is less known than it should be and deserves fuller investigation.*"[54]

Indeed it does; and it is her exhaustive treatment and presentation of *la durée* that lends to her work a richness of tone and profound philosophical significance not usually found in many other contemporary novelists. An acute sensibility and an almost uncanny awareness of the complexity of inner life enables her to present successfully the subjective aspect of human experience. Human life pulsates simultaneously at many levels, each corresponding to a particular ebb or flow of the psychic stream. To believe that these complex aspects of the psyche can lend themselves to a mechanically superimposed notation—the clock—would be a complete misrepresentation of reality. A stream of consciousness novelist is aware of the restrictive nature of language which can flow only in a unilateral forward movement and is incapable of representing the multidirectional nature of *la durée*. This is why Virginia Woolf is inevitably compelled sometimes to state explicitly what she knows cannot be rendered symbolically. This aesthetic dilemma is suggested, if rather crudely, in a scene where Orlando goes out shopping and suddenly hears the clock striking eleven:

"And indeed, it cannot be denied that *the most successful practitioners of the art of life* . . . *somehow contrive to synchronize the sixty or seventy different times which beat simultaneously in every normal human system* so that when eleven strikes, all the rest chime in unison . . . Now as she stood with her hand on the door of her motor-car, the present again struck her on the head. Eleven times she was violently assaulted. 'Confound it all!' she cried, for it is a great shock to the nervous system, hearing a clock strike . . ."[55]

These "successful practitioners of the art of life", or in Bergson's terminology *hommes d'action*, deliberately contrive to resolve into a superficial unity the rich multiplicity of inner life. In our inner duration each moment of experience emerges under the impact of innumerable other moments so that "if there are (at a venture) seventy-six different times ticking in the mind at once, how many different people are there not—Heaven help us—all having lodgment at one time or another in the human spirit?"[56]

This multiplicity behind each commonly conceived unitary self makes personality an eternal process of inter-penetration of different psychic states. The richness and depth of any stream of consciousness, carrying on its surface a mass of recollections and anticipations, lies in this extra-territorial character of each moment responding to its peculiar set of associative images.

The Oak Tree, forming the central unifying thread in the entire narrative covering a period of about three hundred and fifty years, is, in fact, a symbol of evolutionary time. It symbolizes, in the Bergsonian sense, a process of organic growth, the present being eternally recreated by the past into new modes of thought and experience. All the past events in Orlando's life cohere qualitatively into the final pattern that emerges at the end of the novel. His mind, as it develops and

endures[57] through three centuries, grows heavier and heavier
with memories like a weight that we drag up a slope. The
organic development of the poem "The Oak Tree" is symbolical
of this process of creative evolution. When the poem is
finally published, triumphantly reviewed, covetously sought
after by readers and admirers, Orlando decides to bury it
under the age-worn oak tree as a personal record of his-her
spiritual development. Then in a flash the past impinges upon
the present, and she sees the entire range of her experience in
a sudden retrospective vision:

"The ferny path led, with many turns and windings,
higher and higher to the oak tree, which stood on the top.
The tree had grown bigger, sturdier, and more knotted
since she had known it, somewhere about the year 1588 . . .
It was not necessary to faint now in order to look deep into
the darkness where things shape themselves and to see in the
pool of the mind now Shakespeare, now a girl in Russian
trousers, now a toy boat on the Serpentine, and then the
Atlantic itself . . ."[58]

Orlando, therefore, symbolizes the perpetual gnawing of
the past into the present. It is, in the words of a critic, "the
phylogenetic time" incorporating itself "into the ontogenetic
time as one's ancestors are parts of ourselves".[59]

Her next novel, *The Waves* (1931), that followed three
years later, cannot be classified with any of her earlier or later
novels. Exquisite in lyrical composition, rich in poetic
imagery, this novel attempts to communicate an almost
inexpressible fluid impulse behind all human experience. Its
basic intent can again be analysed in terms of durational flux.
Here Virginia Woolf has tried to project time on two
different levels: the normal life-span and the diurnal movement of the sun. On the former level, she treats life in a
pseudo-biographical method employed earlier in *Jacob's
Room*; and on the latter level she presents, through such
symbols as the rise and decline of the sun and waves, a single

day's duration as already shown in *Mrs. Dalloway*. Each phase of the lives of the six characters in the novel corresponds to each of the nine progressive phases of the sun. But these arbitrary divisions should not be taken literally to imply that Virginia Woolf accepts the theory of the Eleatic School and accordingly, presents personality as an assemblage of immobile spatial units. These lunar sections, slicing into bits and thus attempting to regulate life's inner flow, merely expose, as mentioned earlier, the restrictive nature of language and any formal schematization of fluid reality.

"... how tired I am of phrases", says Bernard, "that come down beautifully with all their feet on the ground! Also, how I distrust neat designs of life that are drawn upon half-sheets of note-paper . . . What delights me then is the confusion, the height, the indifference and the fury. Great clouds always changing, and movement . . ."[60] Virginia Woolf, therefore, has to strain hard after creating a sense of fluidity through an appropriate use of words, similes and metaphors. All the six characters often seem to fade into one another (as they "flow and change"[61]) forming, as it were, a larger self into which its components are always merging in a process of qualitative transformation. If Virginia Woolf resorts to the device of "substantive parts"[62] it is only by way of concession to the demands of intelligibility and communication. The world in which Bernard and his friends transmit their inner-most feelings in soliloquized musings is not governed by the clock, its seasons and climates obey other laws, its pulsations are "measured" only by *la durée* which, in Bernard's own words, is a process of "the eternal renewal, the incessant rise and fall and fall and rise again."[63]

The clock which contracts our impulses and sensations is again referred to, in *The Waves*, as an antithesis to *la durée* which is a symbol of inner expansion. "Yes, but suddenly one hears a clock tick. We who had been immersed in this world became aware of another. It is painful. It was Neville who changed our time. He, who had been thinking with the unlimited time of the mind, which stretches in a flash from Shakespeare to ourselves, poked the fire and began to live by that other clock which marks the approach of a particular person. The wide and dignified sweep of his mind contracted. He became on the alert . . . I noted how he touched a cushion. *From the myriads of mankind and all time past he had chosen one person one moment in particular.*"[64]

This is a typical Bergsonian passage in which Virginia Woolf tries to suggest how necessity or action, by focusing the mind on a fixed point of interest ("poked the fire", "touched a cushion") immobilizes its free movement backward and forward in *la durée*. The link with "all time past" is broken, the mind shrinks, is impoverished of its infinite richness and assumes the threadbare vesture of the present moment, a mathematical instant in the ceaseless flow of time.

The Years (1937) may be classified as a period novel, covering a span of about fifty-seven years. It is divided into such arbitrary time-divisions as: Spring 1880, Autumn 1891, Summer 1907, March 1908, Spring 1910, Summer 1911, Winter 1913, Spring 1914, Winter 1917, Autumn 1918 and "Present Day". In style, narration or treatment of time, *The Years* marks no significant development; it is, in fact, in many respects, a regression to the technique of her early novels *The Voyage Out* and *Night and Day*. Devoid of any ostensible sense of *la durée*, this novel remains at most a chronicle of the vicissitudes of the Pargitter family through three generations suggesting, in the background, corresponding changes in the social, political and cultural atmosphere of the times. Of all the characters in this novel, Eleanor alone seems to acquire a certain stature in time, more through a mere accumulation of years than through any spiritual awareness of *le temps perdu*. The chimes of St. Paul in the early pages of the novel appear to be weak imitations of the more meaningful chimes of Big Ben in *Mrs. Dalloway*. Instead of the leaden circles dissolving in the air and striking the hour irrevocable, "the soft circles spread out in the air". [65] Virginia Woolf does, however, even in this novel occasionally suggest the unauthenticity of the clock-time: "But the clocks were irregular, as if the saints themselves were divided. There were pauses, silences . . . Then the clocks struck again." [66]

La durée, which has so far governed the presentation of human experience, now becomes a handmaid to the traditional method of explicit, objective treatment of the passage of time. "The years changed things", announces the narrator, "destroyed things; heaped things up—worries and bothers . . ." [67]

When towards the end Eleanor says, "my life's been other people's lives . . . my father's; Morris's; my friends' lives; Nicholas's", [68] we are reminded of Mrs. Ramsay; but if the old maid pales into insignificance in comparison with "the mother of eight children", it is because she has not grown through *la durée* in which the past endures and not merely superimposes itself upon the present moment.

Between the Acts repeats in a more dramatic form her earlier attempt to represent historic time, covering a period of about three hundred years from the age of Queen Elizabeth to a certain day in June 1939. The interpolated conversations between the acts constitute a novel method of linking the present with the past. Time is thus again stretched backward and forward in an elastic medium. The old theme of the discrepancy between external time and duration is again suggested through Mrs. Swithin's mental meanderings into the historic past, queerly blending with her present perceptions.

". . . she had stretched for her favourite reading—an Outline of History—and had spent the hours between three and five thinking of rhododendron forests in Piccadilly . . . It *took her five seconds in actual time, in mind time ever so much longer,* to separate Grace herself, with blue china on a tray, from the leather-covered grunting monster who was about . . ." [69]

Although unlike Proust Virginia Woolf is not engaged in the recapturing of lost time, nor does she expound explicitly any aesthetic theory in terms of *la durée*, she is, none the less, basically concerned with a similar view of duration and personality. Her characters exist and grow in *la durée*, duration is the sixth sense, the "indwelling servant",[70] the fourth dimension without which their personalities would not emerge in any recognizable form. And when Virginia Woolf denounced the Edwardians as being materialists and urged the younger novelists to capture the spirit Mrs. Brown lived by,[71] she was in fact heralding a new era of fiction in which spatialized rendering of life would give place to a durational representation of human experience.

*   *   *   *   *   *

". . . there is nothing that does not leave some residue, and memory is a light that dances in the mind when the reality is buried," says Virginia Woolf in *The Shooting Party*.[72] In such novels as *Mrs. Dalloway* and *To the Lighthouse* memory does not exist as merely a "residue" but is co-extensive with every perception, immanent as an all-pervasive spirit in every phenomenon. Her use of the stream of consciousness technique, in the middle phase of her literary career, marks the full realization of the importance of memory, particularly *souvenir involontaire*.

Her early novels, *The Voyage Out* and *Night and Day,* deal with the kind of recollections which seem to be only remnants of the traditional "memory digressions". In these novels, Virginia Woolf presents personality as developing along a linear course of chronological sequence, each succeeding phase being more significant than the preceding one, and all events ultimately resolving into a conventional *dénouement,* marriage or death. Characters like Rachel Vinrace, Katherine Hilbery, Hewet or Ralph Denham remain so much engrossed in the present, with only an occasional glimpse of the future, that the past whenever evoked seems to be rather a pleasant emotional diversion than an organic part of their experience. Rachel's love for Hewet or Katherine's for Denham completely obliterates their past, which instead of *enduring* in the present perishes at each instant, making life a mechanical growth and not a process of creative evolution.

In her later novels like *The Years* and *Between the Acts* Virginia Woolf's treatment of memory again lapses into more or less traditional patterns. Eleanor, another "goddess of Time", finds herself occasionally transported into associated memories. For instance, in 1910, at a concert she is reminded of Nicholas by "the fat bouncing young man in his flaxen wig".[73]

Or we have sometimes an instance of "voluntary memory" when two characters engage themselves in a mutual effort to recall a particular experience:

"'I can still see you all sitting round that table, Miss Eleanor', said Crosby. But the table had gone. Morris had taken this; Delia had taken that, everything had been shared out and separated.

'And the kettle that wouldn't boil', said Eleanor, 'D'you remember that'? She tried to laugh.

'Oh, Miss Eleanor', said Crosby, shaking her head, 'I remember everything!'"[74]

But even in such moments, under the inevitable pressure of memories, it is only the present that predominates. "But I've only the present moment, she thought."[75]

Between the Acts is, to borrow Mrs. Swithin's words, an "imaginative reconstruction of the past"[76] in the present perspective. Whereas the acts roll on unfolding the past centuries, the intervening moments are full of social chatter and mild emotional flutters.

It is only in the middle phase of her career, in such novels as *Mrs. Dalloway* and *To the Lighthouse*, that Virginia Woolf becomes increasingly aware of the importance of memory to a literary artist. A careful analysis of these two novels will reveal a very close resemblance between Virginia Woolf on the one hand, and Proust or Bergson on the other, in their treatment of memory. But although she, unlike Proust or Bergson, does not make any clear distinction between the two forms of memory, she does, none the less, address herself frequently to Proust's *souvenir involontaire* or Bergson's *mémoire par excellence*. In *Orlando* we have the first clear exposition of the Bergsonian conception of memory as being a perpetual concomitant of every perception.[77] All experiences are inextricably blended with a medley of associated recollections impinging upon our sensory impressions, thus making our mind a shop-window[78] or a mosaic of very complex design.

". . . nature . . . has further complicated her task and added to our confusion by providing not only a perfect rag-bag of odds and ends within us—a piece of a policeman's trousers lying cheek by jowl with Queen Alexandra's wedding veil—but has contrived that the whole assortment shall be lightly stitched together by a single thread."[79]

She then proceeds to describe memory which always, in Bergson's words, "remains *capricious* in its manifestations".[80] To quote from *Orlando* "*memory is* the seamstress, and a *capricious* one at that. Memory runs her needle in and out, up and down, hither and thither. We know not what comes next, or what follows after . . . Instead of being a single, downright, bluff piece of work of which no man need feel ashamed, our commonest deeds are set about with a fluttering and flickering of wings, a rising and falling of lights."[81]

These recollections keep Orlando in a perpetual glow of emotional flutter so that his whole life becomes a ceaseless stream of associated images and ideas. "And so, the thought of love would be all ambered over with snow and winter; with log fires burning; with Russian women, gold swords, and the bark of stags; with old King James' slobbering . . .

Every single thing, once he tried to dislodge it from its place in his mind, he found thus cumbered with other matter like the lump of glass which, after a year at the bottom of the sea, is grown about with bones and dragonflies, and coins and the tresses of drowned women."[82]

Not only in *Orlando*, but also in such novels as *Mrs. Dalloway* and *To the Lighthouse*, Virginia Woolf makes a consistent presentation of the various aspects of memory. Mrs. Dalloway, at the age of fifty, is like an enormous iceberg whose three-fourths of submerged consciousness occasionally peeps out in the form of associative recollections. In this novel, Virginia Woolf assumes a closer Bergsonian attitude in her frequent blending of pure memory with "learnt recollections", so that it is seldom that we have, like Proust, instances of pure *souvenir involontaire*. Even her seemingly involuntary memories are often blended with an element of contemplation which is less Proustian than Bergsonian in character. For instance, to Peter Walsh, after his brief encounter with Clarissa Dalloway, the chimes of St. Margaret's evoke associated images from their past life,[83] and St. Margaret's itself takes on the form of Mrs. Dalloway. But although the past resurges involuntarily in his mind, its course soon after falls under the directive force of deliberate will in the form of questions:

"It is Clarissa herself, he thought, with a deep emotion, and *an extraordinary clear, yet puzzling, recollection of her, as if this bell had come into the room years ago, where they sat at some moment of great intimacy,* and had gone from one to the other and had left, like a bee with honey, laden with the moment. But what room? What moment? And why had he been so profoundly happy when the clock was striking?"[84]

Compared with Proust, this description is obviously a much feebler attempt at reproducing a past situation through the medium of involuntary memory which also, towards the end, becomes deliberate and self-conscious.

Sometimes a few words may evoke, by association, a past memory in all its original details. Peter Walsh has been snoring on a bench in Regent's Park, near an elderly nurse knitting over a sleeping baby, when suddenly he cries out "the death of the soul"! And at once "the words attached themselves to some scene, to some room, to some past he had been dreaming of. It became clearer; the scene, the room, the past he had been dreaming of".[85] In the following paragraph we start floating along his stream of consciousness:

"It was at Bourton that summer . . . when he was so passionately in love with Clarissa. There were a great many people there, laughing and talking, sitting round a table after tea, and the room was bathed in yellow light and full of cigarette smoke . . . He could see Clarissa now, turning bright pink; somehow contracting . . . 'The death of the soul'. He had said that instinctively, ticketing the moment as he used to do—the death of her soul."[86]

In the course of this vast re-surging of the past, we find Peter Walsh recalling colours, sounds and smells—details both significant and insignificant. For instance, Aunt Helena "sat in her white Cashmere shawl", he remembered, "with her head against the window. And again, "he stood by Miss Parry's chair as though he had been cut out of wood, talking of wild flowers . . ."[87] And finally the vividly remembered scene of his farewell meeting with Clarissa by the fountain "in the middle of a little shrubbery, far from the house, with shrubs and trees all round it. There she came, even before the time, and they stood with the fountain between them, the spout (it was broken) dribbling water incessantly. *How sights fix themselves upon the mind! For example, the vivid green moss.*"[88] In evoking such involuntary memories of the past, Virginia Woolf adopts the same attitude as Bergson in suggesting that once the reel of memory unwinds itself, all the little details, important or unimportant, emerge from their ambush in their true pristine colour and warmth.

This pure memory, says Bergson, "records, in the form of memory-images, all the events of our daily life as they occur in time; it neglects no detail; it leaves to each fact, to each gesture, its place and date. Regardless of utility or of practical application, it stores up the past by the mere necessity of its own nature . . . in it we take refuge every time that, in the search for a particular image, we remount the slope of our past".[89]

To the Lighthouse is designed on a different memory-pattern. Although Mrs. Ramsay, like Mrs. Dalloway, is about fifty, it is not her past that informs the narrative but her present and subsequent "resurrection" in the mind of Lily Briscoe. In the first part of the novel the present expands to reveal, as it were, the infinite possibilities of its impact upon the future; the middle section may be termed—"the storing of memories" through such media as the summer house and the housekeeper; whereas in the last section all these memories unfold themselves in Lily Briscoe's mind enabling her to realize her vision. To bring this vision into proper perspective, she has to put some distance between herself and the canvas.

"Lily stepped back to get her canvas—so—into perspective. It was an odd road to be walking, this of painting. Out and out one went, further and further . . . And as she dipped into the blue paint, she dipped too into the past there. Now Mrs. Ramsay got up, she remembered . . . and there was Minta in front of them with a hole in her stocking . . . The Rayleys, thought Lily Briscoe, squeezing her tube of green paint. She collected her impressions of the Rayleys. Their lives appeared to her in a series of scenes . . ." And thus *she went on tunnelling her way into her picture, into the past*.[90]

There is a close resemblance between Proust's narrator Marcel and Lily Briscoe in their efforts to recapture the past through the medium of art; Marcel through writing his book,[91] and Lily Briscoe through painting her picture. In both cases memory forms the essence underlying all great art. A significant difference between Virginia Woolf and Proust, however, is that like Dorothy Richardson and unlike him, she does not confine herself exclusively to *souvenir involontaire* but moves freely between what Bergson calls the planes of action and pure memory. Like Bergson, she believes in the indestructibility of the past[92] and its power to re-emerge into consciousness with all its infinite details, in the inseparableness of perception from recollection, and the power of memory to project all human experience in true perspective.

✳   ✳   ✳   ✳   ✳   ✳

The polarity of aesthetic forces operating in the novels of Virginia Woolf may be described in terms of *la durée* versus the mathematical instant,[93] becoming versus being, intuition versus intellect. Her experiments in technical procedures, particularly her use of the stream of consciousness, seem to reveal impulses which are rather of a philosophical nature and can be explained better in terms of Bergsonian metaphysics.

Bergson's emphasis on *l'intuition philosophique*[94] as the only authentic approach to the understanding of reality, represents one of the main aesthetic impulses behind the entire work of Virginia Woolf. Endowed with a delicate sensibility, disillusioned by masculine aggressiveness, she presents intuition as co-extensive with femininity, as against the "admirable fabric of the masculine intelligence".[95] That is why it is only her female characters who can act as transparent media for transmitting the living spark of intuition.[96] On the other hand, almost all of her male characters are symbols of pure intellect: William Bankes, the botanist; Charles Tansley who is tracing "the influence of something upon somebody";[97] William Rodney who reads a paper on Shakespeare's imagery; William Pepper who "knew about a great many things—about mathematics, history, Greek, zoology, economics, and the

Icelandic Sagas" and could turn "Persian poetry into English prose, and English prose into Greek iambics";[98] Arthur Ambrose who "spends his life in digging up manuscripts which nobody wants"; Professor Brierly who "knows everything in the whole world about Milton";[99] and Mr. Ramsay "the greatest metaphysician of his time".

These characters, predisposed to abstract analysis, lacking *l'esprit de simplicité* of intuition, are obviously incapacitated from taking a mobile view of reality, since intellect "ne saurait, en général, entrer dans ce qui se fait, suivre le mouvant, adopter le devenir qui est la vie des choses".[100] Intellect is shown here as a destructive force provoking only intellectual skirmishes, and manifesting its uncompromising attitude in sudden egotistical outbursts.

Thought, to a metaphysician, is only a spatial entity, divisible into an infinite number of simultaneities and capable of representing only "points of rest".[101] This provides a clue to the understanding of all male characters in the novels of Virginia Woolf, particularly Mr. Ramsay, whose intellect is compared in a suggestive Bergsonian metaphor to the keyboard of a piano.[102] "For if thought is like the keyboard of a piano, divided into so many notes, or like the alphabet is ranged in twenty-six letters all in order, then his splendid mind had no sort of difficulty in running over those letters one by one, firmly and accurately, until it had reached, say, the letter Q . . . Here, stopping for one moment by the stone urn which held the geraniums, he saw, but now far far away, like children picking up shells, divinely innocent . . . his wife and son, together, in the window."[103]

In this passage Virginia Woolf clearly suggests a contrast between the two conflicting attitudes towards life: the intellectual, as represented by Mr. Ramsay, splitting, dividing, "running over those letters one by one"; and the intuitive, as symbolized by Mrs. Ramsay.[104] Whereas Mr. Ramsay feels "a shutter, like the leathern eyelid of a lizard . . . over the intensity of his gaze",[105] Mrs. Ramsay's intuitive vision pierces through all superficial opacity and penetrates into the inner essence of things. She integrates life, as he disintegrates it. Presiding over the dinner table, she is like a pervasive spirit binding into a mystical unity all the discordant and heterogeneous elements of life, symbolizing the triumph of intuitive love and understanding over intellectual intoleration. "Indeed, she had the whole of the other sex under her protection; for reasons she could not explain . . ."[106]

Mr. Ramsay, on the other hand, was "incapable of untruth; never tampered with a fact; never altered a disagreeable word to suit the pleasure or convenience of any mortal being, least of all of his own children . . . 'But it may be fine—I expect it will be fine', said Mrs. Ramsay . . ."[107]

Mrs. Ramsay, like all Virginia Woolf's female characters, is not a scholar. "Books, she thought, grew of themselves. She never had time to read them."[108] She didn't have to. "She was silent always. She knew then—she knew without having learnt. Her simplicity fathomed what clever people falsified."[109]

It is possible to conceive the relationship between Mr. and Mrs. Ramsay in terms of a Bergsonian analogy. If intellect is matter and intuition *élan vital*, and the action of the latter on the former constitutes the principle of life and evolution, then Mrs. Ramsay is, certainly, the active partner in this relationship. Even the well-known Bergsonian metaphor of the jet of life injecting itself into matter is suggested in the following passage:

"Mrs. Ramsay, who had been sitting loosely, folding her son in her arm, braced herself, and, half-turning seemed to raise herself with an effort, and at once to pour erect into the air a rain of energy, a column of spray, looking at the same time animated and alive as if all her energies were fused into force, burning and illuminating (quietly though she sat, taking up her stocking again), and into this delicious fecundity, this fountain and spray of life, the fatal sterility of the male plunged itself, like a beak of brass, barren and bare. He wanted sympathy. He was a failure, he said . . . It was sympathy he wanted . . . and then to be taken within the circle of life, warmed and soothed, to have his senses restored to him, his barrenness made fertile . . ."[110]

She understands his demand for sympathy instinctively because of the inexplicable advantage of intuition over intellect. "What art was there, known to love or cunning, by which one pressed through those secret chambers? What device for becoming, like waters poured into one jar, inextricably the same, one with the object one adored?"[111] This complete identification with the object is precisely how Bergson defines intuition. It is, he says, that kind of *intellectual sympathy* "by which one places oneself within an object in order to coincide with what is unique in it and consequently inexpressible."[112] It is the same faculty that enables Lily Briscoe to realize, in a flash of inspiration, the vision of her painting, of "the thing itself before it has been made anything."[113]

Mrs. Ramsay has almost the instinct of an insect, a bee for instance, which makes her fathom the secret of human relationship effortlessly. "How then, she had asked herself, did one know one thing or another thing about people, sealed as they were? Only like a bee, drawn by some sweetness or sharpness in the air intangible to touch or taste, one haunted the dome-shaped hive, ranged the wastes of the air over the countries of the world alone, and then haunted the hives with their murmurs and their stirrings; the hives which were people."[114]

This intuitive, almost uncanny, power of apprehension is the hidden secret of Mrs. Ramsay's charm. Endowed with this rare faculty, she has no need to conceptualize reality. She can just take "a look at life, for she had a clear sense of it there, something real, something private, which she shared neither with her children nor with her husband. A sort of transaction went on between them, in which she was on one side, and life was on another . . ."[115]

Instinct is a latent reservoir of knowledge; whereas its external manifestations are often limited to action, it can inwardly reach out to the deepest springs of life and yield secrets otherwise inaccessible even to the greatest intellect. "If the consciousness that slumbers in it should awake, if it were wound up into knowledge instead of being wound off into action", observes Bergson, "if we could ask and it could reply, it would give up to us the most intimate secrets of life."[116]

In Mrs. Ramsay we find a full realization of the potentialities of instinct. She marks the culmination of Virginia Woolf's earlier efforts to represent symbolically the intuitive approach towards life and human relationship. In Mrs. Ramsay are present all those elements which have gone into the making of such earlier characters as Helen Ambrose, Mrs. Hilbery, Mrs. Flanders. In the choice of colours Lily Briscoe is always guided by intuition rather than intelligence. "Now again, moved as she was by *some instinctive need* of distance and blue, she looked at the bay beneath her, making hillocks of the blue bars of the waves, and stony fields of the purpler spaces."[117] Mrs. Dalloway has the instinct of a cat in the understanding of relationships. "Her only gift was knowing people almost by instinct . . . If you put her in a room with some one, up went her back like a cat's, or she purred."[118]

Like Proust, Virginia Woolf believes in the incapacity of the intelligence[119] (the "sterile lucidity" of intellect)[120] to conceive the individual. Intelligence selects from the impressions according to its needs,[121] and is, therefore, incapable of recapturing lost time. "Intuition alone", she would say with Proust, "however tenuous its consistency, however improbable its shape, is a criterion of truth",[122] with Bergson that it is the only method of apprehending mobile reality. Her use

8

of the stream of consciousness, with all its resources of suppleness, flexibility and fluidity, is an indication of her basic intention to present, through intuition, personality in its ceaseless becoming.

*   *   *   *   *   *

"Movement and change are the essence of our being", writes Virginia Woolf in her essay on Montaigne, "rigidity is death; conformity is death."[123]

By immersing herself in her characters' streams of consciousness, Virginia Woolf experiences under the frozen surface of their conventional ego, a state of perpetual flux of which her novels are the most faithful representations. Like Bergson, she conceives thinking as a "continual and continuous change of inward direction".[124] "How fast the stream flows", says Bernard in *The Waves*, "from January to December! We are swept by the torrent of things grown so familiar that they cast no shadow. We float, we float . . ."[125] along this stream of consciousness backward and forward in time.

In the task of representing this fluid reality, a novelist is more happily placed than a metaphysician, since the former, without having to construct it in terms of immutable concepts, is able to suggest it symbolically by employing a suitable method of narrative. In contemporary fiction, the stream of consciousness method of characterization constitutes such an effort to represent symbolically the dynamic aspect of human personality.[126]

However, language, being a spatializing medium, cannot adequately perform the function of suggesting states of consciousness as melting into one another in a process of qualitative organization. It is this aesthetic dilemma that often forces Virginia Woolf into presenting, for mere purposes of intelligibility and communication, psychic states in terms of numerical multiplicity. For instance, when she humorously suggests that there are "seventy-six different times all ticking in the mind at once",[127] she only implies a ceaseless inter-penetration of different states of consciousness.

But to take this numerical expression literally (when the statement clearly suggests a half-serious tone), and interpret her philosophic attitude as conforming to the traditional view of personality as a loose assemblage of discontinuous states, is to completely misunderstand her basic intentions. To quote a contemporary French critic, who prefers to present Virginia Woolf's characters as mixtures of discontinuities and her concept of time as a spatial phenomenon—'désorganis-ation du temps':

"Ces moments vérifient même, parce qu'ils flambent soudain parmi des moments aux lumières différentes, le principe de la discontinuité temporelle: un instant de joie, puis un instant de souffrance . . . la mélodie continue du flot entre dans *le jazz des vagues* . . . Nous sommes tellement asservis à l'espace par la contemplation que nous faisons des 'soixante ou soixante-dix temps différents' que nous pouvons imaginer, 60 ou 70 espaces. Nous divisons ceux-ci, puisqu'ils sont essentiellement divisibles; nous obtenons ces morceaux homogènes que nous appelons instants et que symbolise le 'tic-tic-tic', de l'horloge immobile . . ."[128]

This shows how a critic, predisposed by his philosophical predilections, is likely to misinterpret movement and change as series of immobilities.[129] But in all such cases Virginia Woolf, as if urged instinctively to remove any misunder-standing, throws in the midst of this confusion an unambiguous statement reiterating explicitly her faith in the philosophy of ceaseless flux. For instance, even the passage from *Orlando* quoted above, on which M. Chastaing bases his observations, is followed by a clear description of Orlando's mind as being "fluid that flowed round things and enclosed them com-pletely",[130] as though to link together all seemingly dis-continuous immobilities into a vast movement of perpetual change.

The most emphatic assertion of flux as the ultimate reality forms the theme of one of Louis's soliloquies in which he compares it with the continuous rhythmic movement of a *waltz* and not *jazz* as implied by M. Chastaing:

"I am conscious of flux . . . *It is like a waltz tune*, eddying in and out. The waitresses, balancing trays, swing in and out, round and round . . . *Where then is the break in this continuity?* What the fissure through which one sees disaster? *The circle is unbroken; the harmony complete.* Here is the central rhythm; here the common mainspring. I watch it expand, contract; and then expand again."[131]

This *pulsation éternelle*, in a typical Bergsonian sense, is the creative impulse behind the work of Virginia Woolf. Bernard feels in his dreamy state like "one carried beneath the surface of a stream."[132] "The tree alone resisted", he says in a later soliloquy, *"our eternal flux.* For I changed and changed; was Hamlet, was Shelley, was the hero, whose name I now forget, of a novel by Dostoevsky; was for a whole term, incredibly, Napoleon . . ."[133] Any attempt to regulate this "eternal flux", superimpose an arbitrary design, would be a distortion of reality, for it is a mistake, says Bernard, *"this extreme precision, this orderly and military progress; a convenience, a lie.* There is always deep below it, even when we arrive punctually at the appointed time with our white waistcoats and polite formalities, a rushing stream of broken dreams . . ."[134]

This stream of inner flux flows through all characters, through Mr. Ramsay who is "always changing",[135] through Bernard who is always tormented by "the horrible activity of the mind's eye",[136] through Neville who knows "the person is always changing".[137] The moment Lily Briscoe loses "consciousness of outer things, and her name and her personality and her appearance, and whether Mr. Carmichael was there or not, her mind kept throwing up from its depths, scenes, and names, and sayings, and memories and ideas, like a fountain spurting over . . ."[138]

She experiences this sensation of inner flux more consciously when she had "let the flowers fall from her basket
. . . screwing up her eyes and standing back as if to look at her picture, which she was not touching, however, with all her faculties in a trance, frozen over superficially but moving underneath with extreme speed."[139]

That in rendering such a metaphorical description of the inner flux, Virginia Woolf suggests a close parallelism with Bergson, may be seen from the following extract:

"There is, beneath these sharply cut crystals and this frozen surface, a continuous flux which is not comparable to any flux I have ever seen".[140] (*An Introduction to Metaphysics*)

Another Bergsonian metaphor that occurs frequently in the work of Virginia Woolf likens this inner stream to the swelling of a tune. The melody, according to Bergson, represents perfectly this process of psychic movement:

"Il y a simplement la mélodie continue de notre vie intérieure—mélodie qui se poursuit et se poursuivra, indivisible, du commencement à la fin de notre existence consciente. Notre personnalité est cela même."[141]

In this continuous movement of inner life there are no pauses; perceptions, memories and sensations roll on, as it were, in laval flow, recreating self in eternally new forms. Life, as Virginia Woolf conceives it, is not a predetermined and precisely patterned thing. Since its determining aspect is *la durée*, it has no spatial symmetry or cohesion about it. It is, as she affirms in a famous passage, "not a series of gig lamps symmetrically arranged; life is a luminous halo, a semi-transparent envelope surrounding us from the beginning of consciousness to the end."[142] Such a statement, obviously, implies the supremacy of intuition and flux over logic and determinism.

It matters little whether Virginia Woolf was directly acquainted with Bergson's work or not, nor is it important to assess in this direction her indebtedness to such earlier novelists as Proust, James Joyce and Dorothy Richardson. To attempt to analyse in precise terms the composition of literary genius and resolve it into its components, is a task that has often led literary criticism into bypaths. Our intention in this chapter has been merely to indicate that the basic issues involved in Virginia Woolf's literary theory and practice, particularly her use of the stream of consciousness, are of a philosophical nature and can be most adequately explained in terms of Bergson's view of time and personality. In its rich poetic imagery, tone and rhythmic flow of sentences, and intuitive perception of reality as flux, her work parallels in a remarkable manner the style and philosophic thought of Bergson.

James Joyce

ANY ATTEMPT TO ANALYSE A PRODIGIOUS creative mind like that of Joyce, with a view to finding a single clue to the understanding of his entire work, is not likely to yield any substantial results; for works like *Ulysses* and *Finnegans Wake* encompass in their macro-microcosmic aspect all psychological, philosophical, sociological and scientific attitudes in an effort to render all levels of human experience and consciousness. Each work is a *mélange des genres*: each character, situation or sometimes even word, revolving as it were round a moving point, is a multifaceted phenomenon revealing different meanings at different levels. Psychologists like Jung and Freud;[1] philosophers like Bergson, Berkeley ("Miss Bulkeley"), Alexander; historian-philosophers like Vico and Spengler; anthropologists like Frazer and Levy-Bruhl;[2] scientists like Einstein ("Winestain"), J. W. Dunne and Eddington;[3] the symbolists and the naturalists, to mention only a few, have all contributed towards lending a multi-dimensional significance to his work.

In the face of such a multiplicity of points of view and the vast critical and expository material already available on the various aspects of the work of James Joyce, to put forward any one explanatory theory, however comprehensive in scope, would be a drastic oversimplification. All that is intended here is to show that there are some interesting and illuminating parallels between Bergsonism and some significant aspects of Joyce's technique and attitude.

Wyndham Lewis, one of the earliest critics to suggest this parallelism, failed to inquire into it dispassionately, strongly prejudiced as he was against "Bergson and his school". According to him, Bergson is the devil tempting within his seductive fold all the time-novelists of this century, particularly Joyce, Virginia Woolf, Marcel Proust and Gertrude Stein.

"Without all the uniform pervasive growth of the time-philosophy", writes Wyndham Lewis in *Time and Western Man*, "starting from the little seed planted by Bergson . . . and now spreading more vigorously than ever, there would be no *Ulysses,* or there would be no *A La Recherche du Temps Perdu.* There would be no 'time-composition' of Miss Stein . . ."[4], and he could have added a few years later, no *Finnegans Wake.*

Allowing for some exaggeration and more prejudice in this statement, it is, however, possible to interpret much of Joyce's work in terms of Bergsonian *durée, mémoire par excellence* and intuition.

Unlike Dorothy Richardson, James Joyce's acquaintance with Bergson's thought was neither incomplete nor indirect. He seems to have made an intensive study of the new time-philosophy[5] and realized its importance to the literary artist. There are a few direct and veiled allusions to Bergson in *Finnegans Wake*: he is "Bitchson" against whom Professor Jones, the spatialist, launches his criticism,[6] and together with such other "Celtic" philosophers as Hume, Berkeley and Balfour, he represents in *Exiles*, the philosophical attitude of "incertitude and scepticism" towards life.[7]

In the first quarter of this century, Bergson's thought was attracting the attention of all literary circles in Paris which provided shelter to many a literary exile from other countries.

There was Gertrude Stein who had come in 1914 from Harvard, fully saturated with Jamesian ideas and therefore congenially inclined to understand Bergson's conception of experience as an eternal process of durational flux. There is a certain resemblance between Gertrude Stein's and Joyce's literary technique and general philosophical attitude. Molly Bloom's final monologue seems to resemble in many respects Miss Stein's performance towards the end of *Saints in Seven*. *The Making of Americans* is also a successful rendering of Bergson's theory of ceaseless becoming presented in a style that winds and unwinds itself in an eternal rigmarole of words, phrases and sentences. It is this Jamesian-Bergsonian emphasis on the durational aspect of reality that finds an expression in Stein's literary manifesto in *Composition as Explanation*:

"There is at present there is distribution, by this I mean expression and time, and in this way *at present composition is time* that is the reason that at present . . . the time-sense in the composition is the composition that is making what there is in composition". [8] And again, while explaining the creative impulse behind *Melanctha*, she defines her conception of the "continuous present" as a "constant recurring and beginning". [9]

The present moment in *Ulysses* has the same fluid tendency of continuously fading into the past and future in complete defiance of any arbitrary divisions of time. The minds of Leopold Bloom and Stephen Dedalus remain in a perpetual flux and cannot be said to coincide with any particular "mathematical instant". There is thus a significant resemblance between Joyce's conception of the "continuous present tense", [10] Gertrude Stein's "prolonged present", William James's "specious present", [11] and Bergson's "real, concrete, live present". [12]

Another possible link with Bergson's philosophy is Italo Svevo with whom Joyce lived on terms of close intimacy [13] and whose novels represent Bergsonian theories of time, memory and consciousness.

Ulysses has also been interpreted in terms of symbolism,[14] and through this resemblance related indirectly to Bergsonism.[15] In the course of an analysis of Bergson's influence on Proust, Edmund Wilson suggests how the technique of the French Symbolists implies a metaphysic not very different from Bergson's. The symbolist, he observes, believes that each moment of human experience is essentially conditioned by the mood of the person concerned, the moment and the environments. Each moment thus acquires a new dimension—time. To locate a point one would, therefore, have to seek its co-ordinates not only in space but also in time, which becomes an important determining factor. Thus "the ultimate units of his reality are 'events', each of which is unique and can never recur again—in the flux of the universe . . ."[16]

These remarks may also enable one to grasp one of the fundamental literary and philosophical intentions of James Joyce. In fact, "Joyce is indeed really the great poet of a new phase of the human consciousness", remarks Wilson, his "world is always changing as it is perceived by different observers and by them at different times. It is an organism made up of 'events' . . . and each of these events is unique."[17] These "events" constitute a continuum. We shall have occasion to show later how "events" in *Ulysses* present reality as a dynamic process in which each moment, conditioned by its relative surroundings, is unique. However, to press Joyce's symbolistic technique to the point of establishing an indebtedness to Bergson would hardly yield fruitful results.

Although Joyce, unlike Virginia Woolf, was directly acquainted with Bergson's thought, it does not necessarily imply that his literary experiments show the influence of the philosopher's theories. It would be wrong to presume, like Wyndham Lewis, that without Bergson's influence *Ulysses* could not have been written. Unlike Proust, Joyce makes no reference to Bergson in his *Letters*,[18] nor did he ever acknowledge any such affiliations with the French philosopher. An attempt to trace Bergson's influence on his work would, therefore, be rather far-fetched and even misleading. What is of real importance to note is that Bergson and Joyce, together with all other stream of consciousness novelists, were, as suggested earlier, manifestations of the same *Zeitgeist*. Like Dorothy Richardson's, his acquaintance with Bergson was, in fact, in the nature of a self-realization. If, therefore, an interpretation of his work in terms of Bergsonian *durée*, *mémoire par excellence* and fluid language reveals meanings hitherto unrealized, it is because there exists a marked parallelism between the Bergsonian flux and the stream of consciousness technique as employed by James Joyce.

*　　*　　*　　*　　*　　*

Joyce's experiments with language and technique, indicating his progressive realization of character as a process, culminate in his perfection of the stream of consciousness method of narrative. In attempting to render personality as a ceaseless process of becoming, he achieves far greater success than either Dorothy Richardson or Virginia Woolf. Urged by a prodigious creative impulse to revolt against all accepted literary conventions, he develops, with "the freedom and power of his soul", a view of experience which may be more appropriately described in terms of the Bergsonian conception of life as a river rushing on unimpeded. In *A Portrait of the Artist as a Young Man*, Stephen Dedalus affirms this view of experience:

"How foolish his aim had been! He had tried to build a breakwater of order and elegance against the sordid tide of life without him and to dam up . . . the powerful recurrence of the tides within him. Useless. From without as from within the waters had flowed over his barriers: their tides began once more to jostle fiercely above the crumbled mole."[19]

In fact, the development of James Joyce as an artist can be understood in terms of his increasing awareness of the free creative evolution of personality unimpeded by any utilitarian interests. His preoccupation, therefore, with tides, waves and river-flow, suggested in pictorial or auditory images, is Bergsonian in character.

Young Stephen Dedalus, walking along the beach, listens to "a fourworded wavespeech: seesoo, hrss, rsseeiss, ooos. Vehement breath of waters amid seasnakes . . . It flows purling, widely flowing, floating foampool . . ."[20] The "restlessness of its waves", "the variability of states of sea"[21] constantly haunt his mind. In fact, each of Joyce's characters is conscious of an eternal process of qualitative change and flow, of states of consciousness waxing and waning, interpenetrating each other, ever forming new combinations and seldom repeating themselves mechanically.[22]

It is this Bergsonian view of life that dawns within the consciousness of Leopold Bloom as he walks cheerfully towards "the mosque of the baths", meditating on the kaleidoscopic change of life. "Always passing, the stream of life, which in the stream of life we trace is dearer than them all".[23] And again, while crossing the O'Connell Bridge, his "eyes sought answer from the river" as if to the metaphysical riddle of life itself. "How can you own water really? It's always flowing in a stream, never the same, which in the stream of life we trace. Because *life is a stream*."[24]

In presenting life as a stream "never the same", and personality as a process of dynamic blending of psychic states, Joyce comes nearest to the Bergsonian flux. It may be interesting here to compare Bloom's conception of life with the famous statement of Heraclitus, who is supposed to have anticipated Bergsonian metaphysics as early as 536-470 B.C. To quote from his *Fragments on Nature*:

"Into the same river you could not step twice, for other (and still other) waters are flowing.

To those entering the same river, other and still other waters flow . . .

Into the same river we both step and do not step. We both are and are not."[25]

The fluid method of narrative employed in *Ulysses* is an attempt to represent this conception of life because the streams of consciousness along which Stephen and Bloom float are perpetually renewing their waters, making it impossible for any bygone states to recur mechanically.

It may, however, superficially appear that certain elements do "recur" in the consciousness of Stephen or Bloom: whereas, for instance, the former is obsessed with the feeling that he is responsible for his mother's death, the latter's mind constantly revolves round thoughts of his wife's lover Blazes Boylan, his deceased son Rudy, an undelivered letter to Martha, Dignam's funeral, etc. But a closer analysis will reveal that each moment "recurs" in completely different circumstances, acquiring each time a unique significance of its own. The waters of life thus flow on "in a stream never the same", each drop coalescing with the next, forming new combinations in a process of creative renewal. In a similar sense, the human mind remains in a state of perpetual flux, jumping across all boundaries of time and space, changing and growing in a medium that could be called *la durée*.

Bloom, as he listens to the discussions of the young medical students in the National Maternity Hospital, experiences this dynamism of the human soul in its power to transcend all chronological sequence and flow freely into the past and future:

"What is the age of the soul of man? As she hath the virtue of the chameleon to change her hue at every approach . . . No longer is Leopold, as he sits there, ruminating, chewing the cud of reminiscence, that staid agent of publicity and holder of a modest substance in the funds. He is young Leopold, as in a restrospective arrangement, a mirror within a mirror . . ."[26]

With this resurge within his mind, like Marcel's remembrances of the days of childhood, experiences of infancy when he used to walk every morning to the school: "his booksatchel on him bandolierwise, and in it a goodly hunk of wheaten loaf, a mother's thought".[27] And together with this recollection other memories crowd in upon his mind, intermingling with one another, like the different colours of a rotating prism. The stream of thought flows on, carrying on its surface recollections and visions, "all their moving moaning multitude . . ."[28] All thoughts blend and fuse, and then emerges from this chaos, as though by a stroke of metamorphosis, the vision of the everlasting bride Martha, coifed with a veil of gossamer which "flows about her starborn flesh and loose it streams emerald . . ."[29] And so the human mind moves on in a presentational continuum, undergoing psychic metamorphosis every moment. No contemporary novelist has represented more successfully than James Joyce what may be termed Bergson's "philosophy of change", or internal movement and perpetual becoming. His preoccupation with rivers and streams indicates his affirmation of this notion of experience.

"I love rivers", Joyce once remarked to Louis Gillet, and "all which flows",[30] and to pay his homage, as it were, to the river Liffey he wrote the 'Anna Livia Plurabelle' episode in *Finnegans Wake*.[31]

Ulysses has been rightly called by Marcel Thiebault "un film de conscience", by Harry Levin a "*roman fleuve*",[32] by Edouard Dujardin "une projection cinématographique",[33] which recalls to one's mind Bergson's famous analogy of the movement implicit in a cinematograph film as being most representative of the quick succession in our states of consciousness. Emphasizing the qualitative aspect of cinematographic interpenetration, Bergson points out the fallacy of conceiving experience as an assemblage of discrete, separate snapshots. "We take snapshots, as it were, of the passing reality", he says in *Creative Evolution*, "and, as these are characteristic of the reality, we have only to string them on a becoming, abstract, uniform and invisible, situated at the back of the apparatus of knowledge, in order to imitate what there is that is characteristic in this becoming itself."[34]

On the other hand reality, according to Bergson, is synonymous with the qualitative interpenetration of these static snapshots into each other. It is this cinematographic nature of human consciousness that forms the basis of the stream of consciousness method employed by James Joyce in *Ulysses*; and its most successful illustration is the final monologue of Molly Bloom which may be rightly described as "le flux ininterrompu des pensées".[35] The last forty-four pages of this novel, unpunctuated, letting words run on in an unprecedented flow, provide an adequate example of Bergson's description of experience as one long uninterrupted sentence.

". . . suppose that my speech had been lasting for years, since the first awakening of my consciousness, that it had been carried on in one single sentence, and that my consciousness were sufficiently detached from the future, disinterested enough in action . . . Well, I believe that *our whole psychical existence is something just like this single sentence,* continued since the first awakening of consciousness, interspersed with commas, but never broken by full stops."[36]

James Joyce suggests in Molly Bloom's monologue the fluid nature of our psychic life as "something just like this single sentence" unbroken by full stops, not even "interspersed with commas", in order to represent the true nature of consciousness. In a sense, *Ulysses* itself is one such long sentence attempting to render in a literary medium the mobile contours of reality.

Mrs. Bloom's *film de conscience* projects on the reader's mind scenes from her past life, in a cinematographic succession, blending indiscriminately dramatic love experiences with insignificant details as they issue out of the latent reservoir of "pure memory":

". . . she gave me the Moonstone to read that was the first I read of Wilkie Collins East Lynne I read and the shadow of Ashlydyat Mrs Henry Wood Dunbar by that other woman I lent him afterwards with Mulveys photo in it so as he see I wasnt without and Lord Lytton Eugene Aram Molly bawn she gave me by Mrs Hungerford on account of the name I don't like books with a Molly in them . . . this blanket is too heavy on me thats better I havent even one decent nightdress this thing gets all rolled up under me besides him . . ."[37]

And so rolls on this mighty avalanche of memories, perceptions and thoughts, with scarce a punctuation mark to impede its dynamic flow. Dormant instincts and impulses emerge in their pristine colour and flow along a course of free association. Perhaps no other single passage in contemporary literature would provide a more apt illustration of what Bergson considers the intrinsic nature of all living thought and the defining feature of "the whole art of writing".

In his essay "The Soul and the Body", Bergson expounds at some length his theory of literary composition. If we dispense with all artificial renderings of thought, we shall be confronted with directions rather than states, because thinking is primarily an endless change of inward direction. A writer's purpose should be to suggest, as far as possible, these "comings and goings of the mind". In order to catch our thought in its nascent state and "make it pass, still living, into the soul of another", it is imperative that every writer should choose words and arrange them in such patterns as to bring out the latent dynamism in our mental processes. The words "will not convey the whole of what we wish to make them say", adds Bergson, "if we do not succeed by the rhythm . . . by a particular dancing of the sentence, in making the reader's mind, continually guided by a series of nascent movements, describe a curve of thought and feeling analogous to what we ourselves describe. *In this consists the whole art of writing.*"[38]

Mrs. Bloom's monologue demonstrates not only the true nature of our consciousness in its ceaseless change of inward direction, but by completely dispensing with punctuation, goes a step further towards representing in verbalized form thought as unadulterated by any "artificial reconstructions". *Ulysses* and *Finnegans Wake* do show that language, in spite of being a spatial medium, can render to a remarkable degree experience as flux and personality as an eternal process of becoming.

Anna Livia Plurabelle repeats, in many respects, the earlier performance of Molly Bloom in representing personality as a process. In fact, she is a most effective symbol of Bergsonian flux, perpetually changing into different forms, to one state constant never. She undergoes continuous metamorphosis, becomes Isis, Iseult, a floating cloud, a running stream and innumerable other forms, aerial or solid, human or inanimate. In brief, she represents the principle underlying Bergson's creative energy manifesting itself in diverse forms, the multi-faceted reality itself. As Finnegan's widow she "sprids the boord", as Isis she collects the remnants of the dismembered body of Osiris, her brother-husband; as mother-hen Belinda she digs out of a rubbish heap a letter that baffles with its mysterious intent all scholarly interpreters.

But she is primarily the river Liffey that flows on, winding its course from the Wicklow Hills, running past the Chapelizod of Earwicker's pub, singing *"I'se so silly to be flowing but I no canna stay!"*[39] Her essence is ceaseless change, her life is flux. Towards the end of this enigmatic saga of the rise and fall of man, Anna Livia Plurabelle recalls in a retrospective vision, like Mrs. Bloom, her experiences of bygone days which flash past her mind in a cinematograph film, blending one image into another in an onrush of words:

"The day. Remember! Why there that moment and us two only? I was but teen, a tiler's dot. The swankysuits was boosting always, sure him, he was like to me fad . . . I'm sure he squirted juice in his eyes to make them flash for flightening me . . . I was the pet of everyone then. A princeable girl. And you were the pantymammy's Vulking Corsergoth. The invision of Indelond. And, by Thorror, you looked it! My lips went livid for from the joy of fear. Like almost now. How? How you said how you'd give me the keys of me heart. And we'd be married till delth to uspart. And though dev do espart. O mine! Only, no, now it's me who's got to give."[40]

Except that Joyce has retained punctuation and to that extent stemmed the uninterrupted flow of sentences, he has here repeated the earlier performance of Mrs. Bloom. And whatever effect of fluidity he may have thus lost through the use of commas and full-stops, he has amply made up by smelting words into new protean shapes, and thereby reenacting the "genesis and mutation of language". His intention is to let letters and words fade into multiversant combinations and thus present experience as a dynamic phenomenon.

In this respect he is more Bergsonian than either Dorothy Richardson or Virginia Woolf, whose literary experiments are confined exclusively to formal verbalizations of their characters' streams of consciousness. Joyce, in penetrating beneath the "frozen surface" of "sharply cut crystals",[41] into the regions of subliminal consciousness, is able to experience the inner flux more successfully than any other stream of consciousness novelist, and present this phenomenon in a new fluid language of his own invention.

Anna Livia Plurabelle's polymorphous "untitled mamafesta" is as fluid as her own consciousness. It does not symbolize any "rigid and ready-made concepts" but embodies "supple, mobile and almost fluid representations"[42] of man's eternally changing attitudes towards life. "The proteiform graph itself is a polyhedron of scripture . . . Closer inspection of the *bordereau* would reveal a multiplicity of personalities . . ."[43] *"every person, place and thing in the chaosmos of* Alle *anyway* connected with the gobblydumped turkery *was moving and changing every part of the time*: the travelling inkhorn (possibly pot), the hare and turtle pen and paper, the continually more and less intermisunderstanding minds of the anti-collaborators, then as time went on as it will variously inflected, differently pronounced, otherwise spelled, changeably meaning vocable scriptsigns". [44] In a sense, the entire work is a symbol of "the constant of fluxion". [45] *"The Fin had a flux."* [46]

*   *   *   *   *   *

Joyce's experiments in the "laboratory of the word" [47] in collaboration with such other literary associates as Stuart Gilbert, Eugene Jolas, Jean Paulhan, Justinus Kerner, Raymond Queneau, in giving "back to language its pre-logical functions", [48] in exposing "the hoary imbecility of 'correct English'," [49] though not directly inspired by Bergson's theory of language, can, none the less, be interpreted in terms of Bergsonism. It is difficult to conjecture how Bergson might have reacted to the new experiments in writing, but a close study of his observations on the nature and use of language will reveal an intimate resemblance of aesthetic intention.

Bergson, like Joyce, reiterates that the conventional word—"the trim trite truth letter" [50]—recognizes only the most commonplace aspect of things and is capable of representing only the Form and not Change. [51] It is like a spatial entity existing in a homogeneous medium and implies an inevitable solidification of our fluid impressions. "In the same way as the fleeting duration of our ego is fixed by its projection in homogeneous space, our constantly changing impressions, wrapping themselves round the external object which is their cause, take on its definite outlines and its immobility." [52] With regard to sensations, Bergson further adds, "not only does language make us believe in the unchangeableness of our sensations, but it will sometimes deceive us as to the nature of the sensation felt."[53] Hence his call to the novelist to penetrate into the depths of our superficial ego symbolized by the conventional word, and represent qualitative inter-penetration of states of consciousness.[54]

In response, as it were, to a similar call to represent *l'émotion créatrice* in its mobile contours and with "the least possible shrinkage", Joyce feels constrained to forge in the smithy of his soul a new notation for rendering the fleeting nuances of human emotions. But such experimentation may often result in blocking the normal channels of communication. A novelist who, in spite of these insurmountable difficulties, pursues relentlessly his aesthetic ideal of transcribing reality as faithfully as possible would have to try bold and ingenious experiments with language. Such a *"writer will attempt to realize the unrealizable"*.[55]

James Joyce is essentially engaged in this effort to penetrate into the hard crust of the conventional word, seize it in its embryonic form and then remould it to embody nascent movements in his characters' streams of conscious-ness. It is not our intention here to present a detailed analysis of the various linguistic devices employed by him to achieve the effect of involuntary fluidity. We are concerned only with suggesting the main aesthetic and philosophic impulses behind his linguistic-experiments.

In *The Two Sources of Morality and Religion*, Bergson seems to justify these linguistic experiments of James Joyce, whose style is a myriad-tinted spectrum, a process of inward direction, and not an immobile substratum of centuries of conventional thinking:

"Anyone engaged in writing has been in a position to feel the difference between an intelligence left to itself and that which burns with the fire of an original and unique emotion, born of the identification of the author with his subject, that is to say of intuition. In the first case the mind cold-hammers the materials, combining together ideas long since cast into words and which society supplies in a solid form. In the second, it would seem that the solid materials supplied by intelligence first melt and mix, then solidify again into fresh ideas now shaped by the creative mind itself. If these ideas find words already existing which can express them, for each of them this seems a piece of unexpected good luck; and, in truth, it has often been necessary to assist fortune, and strain the meaning of a word, to mould it to the thought. In that event the effort is painful and the result problematical. But it is in such a case only that the mind feels itself, or believes itself, to be creative. It no longer starts from a multiplicity of ready-made elements to arrive at a composite unity made up of a new arrangement of the old. It has been transported at a bound to something which seems both one and unique, and which will contrive later to express itself, more or less satisfactorily, in concepts both multiple and common, previously provided by language."[56]

Joyce's bold experiments with language are obviously actuated by "an original and unique emotion". His mind, dispensing with the traditional mode of cold-hammering the materials, forges a new notation of expression to represent aesthetic experience in its nascent freshness and entirety. Words are for Joyce living organisms: they pour in as mysterious messages from the Eucharist, as young Stephen Dedalus walks through the streets of Dublin with his eyes and ears ready to receive fleeting impressions.[57] After his narrow escape from a street brawl in Night-town, as he listens to Bloom's monotone he "could hear, of course, all kinds of words changing colour like those crabs about Ringsend in the morning . . ."[58]

The monologues of Molly Bloom and Anna Livia Plurabelle are examples of dynamic consciousness flowing in a stream. Joyce's words, like Bergson's hypothetical fluid concepts, can bend, turn and coil round objects and meanings to render the effect of mobile reality. In the conventional style, each sentence is a unit with a single meaning running through words, but in Joyce's sentences, each word is loaded with associative overtones, making his sentences multifluvian streams of superimposed meanings interpenetrating each other in a qualitative process of flux. The classic example of this form of writing is the last sentence of *Finnegans Wake* ("A way a lone a last a loved a long the") which flows into the opening sentence ("riverrun, past Eve and Adam's, from swerve of shore to bend of bay, brings us by a commodius vicus of recirculation back to Howth Castle and Environs"[59]).

＊　＊　＊　＊　＊　＊

Except *Dubliners*, each one of Joyce's works is, in a sense, "a retrospective arrangement" of his own past experience, a quest like Proust's after the essence of time. Whereas the *Portrait* and *Ulysses* treat time as *durée réelle*, as a process of interblending of the past, present and future, *Finnegans Wake* attempts to present the entire historical consciousness of man.

Memory forms in the work of Joyce, as of Proust, the basis of art. Proust, remarks Wyndham Lewis, "*returned* to the *temps perdu.* Joyce never left it. He discharged it as freshly as though the time he wrote about were still present, because it was *his* present."[60]

Joyce is primarily engaged in an attempt to relive his past away from the locale and recreate it in a medium that may be called *la durée*. In an effort to recapture the past through his characters, Joyce only affirms the principle of continuity in all experience. Young Dedalus notes in his diary of April 6 that "the past is consumed in the present and the present is living only because it brings forth the future."[61]

To fully grasp the impulse behind Joyce's art of characterization, the reader must immerse himself in the character's stream of consciousness to realize the slow process of becoming in which he is ceaselessly involved. The past, in a typical Bergsonian sense, has no separate identity as such; it forms an organic part of the ever swelling *durée*. The present, therefore, if at all we could segregate time into mechanical divisions, is constantly growing into larger dimensions in a process of change. This explains Stephen's reaction to Bloom's "unfamiliar melody" (in the Ithaca episode) in which he hears "the accumulation of the past."[62]

Each of his characters lives in a twilight zone of past association and immediate perceptions, particularly in moments of heightened sensibility when the mind (remarks Stephen Dedalus) "is a fading coal, that which I was is that which I am and that which in possibility I may come to be."[63]

Stephen and Bloom live under a perpetual shadow of the past; they are paragons of memory. "My memory's not so bad",[64] says Bloom, and so could Stephen Dedalus and Molly Bloom justly pride themselves on their vivid remembrances of things past. They do not go, like Proust's Marcel, in search of lost time: memory is co-extensive with their perceptions, manifesting itself in a thousand elusive forms. It may, in fact, be said that *mémoire involontaire* is a permanent aspect of their mental processes, and it is rarely that they have to evoke past images by a deliberate effort of the will. When Stephen Dedalus, under a somewhat embarrassing thrust from his rival Heron, begins to recite the *Confiteor*, he hears both Heron and Wallis breaking into laughter:

"The confession came only from Stephen's lips and, while they spoke the words, *a sudden memory had carried him to another scene called up, as if by magic*, at the moment when he had noted the faint cruel dimples at the corners of Heron's smiling lips . . ."[65]

These "magical" recurrences of the past images are, in fact, a permanent feature of the stream of consciousness method as employed by Joyce. These recollections come in parts, as disconnected images, half-remembered words and phrases, and float along the stream of thought.

"Stream of life. What was the name of that priestylooking chap was always squinting in when he passed? Weak eyes, woman. Stopped in Citron's saint Kevin's parade. Pen something . . . Of course it's years ago. Noise of the trams probably . . ."[66]

In order to represent the ceaseless flow of involuntary memory, Joyce often presents past images in a strangely jumbled form. Bloom's "retrospective arrangements", for instance, are invariably of this nature:

"Bloowho went by Moulang's pipes, bearing in his breast the sweets of sin, by Wine's antiques in memory bearing sweet sinful words, by Carroll's dusky battered plate, for Raoul."[67]

Or again, "Long day I've had. Martha, the bath, funeral, house of keys, museum with those goddesses, Dedalus' song. Then that bawler in Barney Kiernan's . . ."[68]

It is not difficult to trace in these extracts overtones from Leopold Bloom's experiences earlier in the day and his pre-occupations with thoughts of his wife's lovers and the nostalgic memories of his deceased son. These memories rise and fall, uncontrolled by any conscious will, and are therefore flashes of "pure memory" which records faithfully all occurrences in their original details, assigning "to each fact, to each gesture, its place and date".[69] This may be illustrated by another extract from Ulysses:

"Windy night that was I went to fetch her . . . He and I behind. Sheet of her music blew out of my hand against the high school railings . . . Remember her laughing at the wind, her blizzard collar up . . . Remember when we got home raking up the fire and frying up those pieces of lap of mutton for her supper with the Chutney sauce . . . Could see her in the bedroom from the hearth unclamping the busk of her stays. White . . . Swish and soft flop her stays made on the bed . . . That was the night . . ."[70]

It is interesting to note how Bloom's mind has been able to retain across many years even such minor details as the "pieces of mutton" and "swish and soft flop" of his wife's stays.

Joyce's next concern is to suggest the source of these involuntary recollections and in this respect he again presents a Bergsonian view of memory. This problem occupies Stephen Dedalus' mind during his rambles at Clongowes in the company of his father:

"His monstrous reveries came thronging into his memory. They too had sprung up before him, suddenly and furiously, out of mere words. He had soon given in to them and allowed them to sweep across and abase his intellect, *wondering always where they came from, from what den of monstrous images . . .*"[71]

This den whence issue these "monstrous reveries" is, as already suggested, Bergson's "pure memory" which registers alongside of each other all events in their original order of sequence. From this reservoir emerge, voluntarily or involuntarily, depending upon the state of our mental tension at a particular moment, past images in response to stimuli from our immediate environments.

Joyce's treatment of memory is as significant as Proust's, though not as comprehensive. He is impelled by a similar urge to recognize the importance of involuntary memory in prose-fiction. The most significant passage on memory occurs in *Ulysses* where Mrs. Mina Purefoy, the wife of the accountant of the Ulster bank, is lying in child-bed and recalls "across the mist of years" memories of her smooth marital relations with her husband, "*memories*[72] which are hidden away by man in the darkest places of the heart but *they abide there and wait.* He may suffer their memory to grow dim, let them be as though they had not been and all but persuade himself that they were not or at least were otherwise. *Yet a chance word will call them forth suddenly* and they will rise up to confront him in the most various circumstances, a vision or a dream, or while timbrel and harp soothe his senses . . . A scene disengages itself in the observer's memory, evoked, it would seem, by a word of so natural a homeliness as if those days were really present there (as some thought) with their immediate pleasures. A shaven space of lawn one soft May evening, the wellremembered grove of lilacs at Roundtown, purple and white", [73] in fact any seemingly insignificant object is likely to bring back to one's mind an entire past experience.

In tone and presentation, this passage will recall Bergson's theory of memory, or Proust's treatment of *mémoire involontaire* in *A la recherche du temps perdu*. [74] Not only does this passage provide a comprehensive answer to Stephen's query with regard to the nature and origin of memories but it also supplies an important clue to the understanding of much of the work of James Joyce. The passage opens with an affirmation of the indestructibility of the past, of the dictum that memories may lie dormant in the unconscious but they only "abide there and wait". This eternal existence of our past is one of the fundamental tenets of Bergson's conception of "pure memory" as, according to him, each moment is characterized by "a persistence of the past in the present". [75]

In the second half of the passage Joyce proceeds to illustrate further his theory of memory by showing how a single chance word, scene or object may evoke in us a past experience which otherwise might seem to have faded into complete oblivion. Memory, therefore, for both Joyce and Proust, is central to the understanding of the true nature of human consciousness: it is synonymous with duration in which the self is constantly growing into new forms in a process of creative evolution. Stephen Dedalus appears to represent this Bergsonian view of experience when he describes his ceaseless metamorphosis into new selves:

"Wait. Five months. Molecules all change. I am other I now . . .

But I, entelechy, form of forms, *am I by memory because under everchanging forms* . . ." [76]

One may not agree with Wyndham Lewis's assertion that the "powerful impressionism of *Ulysses*" and "the mental method" employed by Joyce date "from the publication of *Matière et Mémoire*."[77] Yet there exists a marked parallelism in view of the close resemblance between Joyce's treatment of memory and Bergson's.

* * * * * *

Although the aesthetic theory of Stephen Dedalus is "in the main applied Aquinas"[78] with a few tags of "Aristotle's poetics and psychology",[79] it is possible to interpret it in terms of Bergsonism.

In the course of a scholarly exposition to Lynch of his conception of beauty, Stephen cites *integritas*, *consonantia* and *claritas* as its three main attributes, corresponding to the three necessary phases of artistic apprehension. *Integritas* implies that each aesthetic image is apprehended as "selfbounded and self-contained upon the immeasurable background of space or time which is not it".[80] Then we pass on to the next phase of artistic apprehension, *consonantia*, which signifies a rhythmic relationship between the various parts constituting the image. In brief, an integral perception is succeeded by "the analysis of apprehension". *Claritas*, the third attribute of beauty, Stephen admits, is at best a rather vague and inexact term, but he proceeds to interpret it as "the scholastic *quidditas* . . . the clear radiance of the esthetic image . . . apprehended luminously by the mind which has been arrested by its wholeness and fascinated by its harmony . . ."[81] This supreme aspect of beauty resembles, in certain respects, Bergson's *l'intuition philosophique* which enables a person to enter into the heart of an aesthetic image and apprehend it, in a single effort, as a rhythmic synthesis of its organically related components.

Let us now examine the first two essentials of beauty: *integritas* and *consonantia* in terms of Bergson's aesthetic. In one of his most illuminating essays entitled "Intellectual Effort" Bergson, like Stephen Dedalus, describes the different phases of artistic awareness. [82] According to him, every artist first conceives his subject as a whole scheme or apprehends his aesthetic image, to borrow Stephen's terminology, as *integritas* and then proceeds to realize it analytically as comprising parts related in a harmonious relationship. The entire progression in the process of literary composition is thus from "scheme to image". [83]

"It must necessarily be assumed, then", observes Bergson, "that the whole is presented as a scheme, and that invention consists precisely in converting the scheme into image", in realizing the rhythmic relationship between parts constituting the whole. [84] He then proceeds to illustrate his aesthetic theory:

"The author writing a novel, the dramatist creating his characters and situations, the musician composing a symphony, the poet composing an epic, all have in mind, first of all, something simple and abstract, something, so to say, incorporeal. For the musician and poet it is a new impression, which they must unfold in sounds or in imagery. For the novelist and the dramatist it is a theme to be developed into events, a feeling, individual or social, to be materialized in living personages. They start with a scheme of the *whole*, and the end is obtained when they reach a distinct image of the *elements*." [85]

The "end" signifies here nothing else than an apprehension of the aesthetic image as "the result of its parts and their sum, harmonious. That is *consonantia*." [86]

Consonantia, Stephen further implies, is the passing from one element to another, till all is held together in a balance and one feels "the rhythm of its structure". It is the same rhythmic essence underlying every work of art, hidden behind its various parts, to which Bergson refers in his essay "The Life and Work of Ravaisson":

"True art aims at portraying the individuality of the model and to that end it will seek behind the lines one sees the movement the eye does not see, behind the movement itself something even more secret, the original intention, the fundamental aspiration of the person: a simple thought equivalent to all the indefinite richness of form and colour."[87]

The "simple thought" behind the multiplicity of lines and curves represents the "scheme" or integral apprehension of the aesthetic image. When the beholder of a beautiful object realizes this basic impulse, his response may be likened to "that cardiac condition which", cites Stephen, "the Italian physiologist Luigi Galvani . . . called the enchantment of the heart".[88] This attribute of beauty, says Stephen, is *claritas*. It may be seen that *claritas* bears a certain resemblance to Bergson's *l'intuition philosophique*, with the only difference that whereas the former is the culmination of the two preceding phases—*integritas* and *consonantia*—the latter signifies an immediate identification with the image to realize it in its entirety.

This resemblance between Stephen's aesthetic and Bergson's assumes still more significant proportions when the former elaborates his theory of art as progressing through three distinct forms: the lyrical, the epical and the dramatic.[89] These forms of art, as we shall now try to indicate, can be interpreted in terms of a progressive awareness of aesthetic experience from its being a loose assemblage of discrete emotions to its realization as a process of fluid continuity.

The lyrical form, it may be seen, represents, according to Stephen Dedalus, the most elementary phase of literary creation, being in fact "the simplest verbal vesture of *an instant of emotion*, a rhythmical cry such as ages ago cheered on the man who pulled at the oar or dragged stones up a slope. He who utters it is more conscious of the instant of emotion than of himself as feeling emotion."[90] In other words, every lyrical outburst of feeling remains a discrete and independent entity not completely related to the person who experiences it. This, according to Bergson, would be symbolical of a mechanistic conception of experience constituting instants of emotion as spatial elements not lending themselves to a process of creative interpenetration of the "instant of emotion" and the artist "himself as feeling emotion". This marks the first stage in the development of artistic modes of expression, and the epical form emerges from it "when the artist prolongs and broods upon himself as the centre of an epical event". The unrelated instant of emotion has now lengthened itself into "an epical event", and the artist by virtue of prolonged brooding upon himself, is able to let his personality flow into his work, giving to the experience therein represented a dynamic aspect. To quote Stephen Dedalus again, "the personality of the artist passes into the narration itself, flowing round and round the persons and the action like a vital sea."[91]

The dramatic form, Stephen further adds, "is reached when the vitality which has flowed and eddied round each person fills every person with such *vital force* that he or she assumes a proper and intangible esthetic life. The personality of the artist, at first a cry or a cadence or a mood and then a fluid and lambent narrative, finally refines itself out of existence, impersonalizes itself, so to speak. The esthetic image in the dramatic form is life purified in and reprojected from the human imagination."[92] This is how, he concludes, "the mystery of esthetic, like that of material creation", is consummated.

This seems to be an interesting counterpart to Bergson's theory of creative evolution in which the dramatic form signifies the culmination of the *élan vital* ("vital force") injecting itself into matter and transforming it into living organism. The dramatic form implies, however paradoxical it may seem, the immanence of the creative spirit in every character or situation. The artist, through a stupendous intuitive effort, succeeds so completely in identifying himself with his character and scene that he remains, like God Almighty, "within or behind or beyond or above his handi-work, invisible, refined out of existence . . ."[93] This attitude of the dramatic artist is often misunderstood to signify conventional objectivity, whereas it implies, in fact, the culmination of the literary process when the artist, after having injected something of his *élan vital* into each of his characters, finally emerges as a cosmic spirit, "indifferent, paring his fingernails".

Joyce's own development as a novelist may be explained in terms of these progressive forms of literary composition. *Stephen Hero* and *A Portrait of the Artist as a Young Man* represent the earliest phase of literary development, both novels being, in a sense, a series of discrete instants of emotion or rhythmical cries, not cohering into any ostensible pattern of dynamic continuity. The main episode in the *Portrait*, when Stephen in the course of his rambles on the beach suddenly realizes his aesthetic ideal of using words in their multiple meanings and associations, centres round an intense lyrical cry of spiritual anguish. "His throat ached with a desire to cry aloud, the cry of a hawk or eagle on high, to cry piercingly of his deliverance to the winds . . . An instant of wild flight had delivered him and the cry of triumph which his lips withheld cleft his brain.—Stephaneforos!"[94]

As he breaks away in freedom from "the pale service of the altar", he feels "his throat throbbing with song . . . a lust of wandering in his feet", and a few paces further, his eyes fall on a girl whose "bosom was as a bird's, soft and slight, slight and soft as the breast of some darkplumaged dove . . . Heavenly God! cried Stephen's soul, in an outburst of profane joy."[95]

These moments of lyrical intensity, like discrete drops of water, seem to become larger and heavier and then fall down without flowing into a continuous stream.

Ulysses emerges from the *Portrait* as Joyce "prolongs and broods upon himself as the centre of an epical event".[96] The narrative ceases to be a mere pseudo-biography, with the centre of interest shifting from Stephen Dedalus to Leopold Bloom. But Joyce's vicarious experience appears to flow round each of his characters and episodes like "a vital sea". *Ulysses*, unlike the *Portrait*, is not a series of lyrical outbursts, but progresses organically with an epical design imposed upon its continuous flow. Leopold Bloom's commonplace experiences of a single day have the same epical significance as the adventures of Ulysses, his Greek prototype. *Ulysses*, in a sense, is a vast epic of the Common Man of today.

But Stephen Dedalus in *Ulysses* still strongly suggests the personal point of view of his creator, and therefore, it is only in *Finnegans Wake* that Joyce completely refines himself "out of existence" and achieves an impersonal presentation of experience. In this sense, *Finnegans Wake* is a "dramatic" work, because the writer's personality does not intrude into the narrative which flows on, as it were, by itself. Characters and situations, mythical or symbolical, culled from the summation of human experience, blend ceaselessly into each other in a process of "constant fluxion".

*   *   *   *   *   *

Stuart Gilbert, in his essay "Art and Intuition", quotes Dr. Wildon Carr's definition of intuition as "an activity which characterizes. It gives us a knowledge of things in their concreteness and individuality."[97]

This concept of intuition as a mysterious faculty of knowing objects seems to correspond, in certain respects, with what Stephen Dedalus designates as "epiphany". He mentions it as the third attribute of beauty, synonymous with *claritas*.

"After the analysis which discovers the second quality", Stephen explains to his friend Cranly,[98] "the mind makes the only logically possible synthesis and discovers the third quality. This is the moment which I call epiphany. First we recognize that the object is *one* integral thing, then we recognize that it is an organized composite structure, a *thing* in fact: finally, when the relation of the parts is exquisite, when the parts are adjusted to the special point, we recognize that it is *that* thing which it is. Its soul, its whatness, leaps to us from the vestment of its appearance. The soul of the commonest object, the structure of which is so adjusted, seems to us radiant. The object achieves its epiphany."[99]

On a close analysis, this concept of epiphany suggests, in many respects, Bergson's *l'intuition philosophique* which enables us to have an instantaneous apprehension of an object.[100] Epiphany and intuition may, however, appear to differ from each other in two respects: first, whereas the former is a phenomenon, the latter is a faculty; secondly, whereas epiphany is the outcome of *integritas* and *consonantia*, intuition implies, on the other hand, an immediate identification with the image or object without any intermediary stages. But on further examination even this apparent difference becomes insignificant. If an object "achieves its epiphany", it is only in the mind of the beholder who perceives it in an intuitive flash. And even Bergson recognizes, however grudgingly, in his concept of intuition "une imprégnation graduelle" or an "effort préalable" before "la complication diminue. Puis les parties entrent les unes dans les autres. Enfin tout se ramasse en un point unique . . ."[101]

The emphasis, however, in both cases is on the *sudden* revelation of an unexpected aspect of an object or experience. In the words of the narrator, "by an epiphany he meant *a sudden spiritual manifestation*, whether in the vulgarity of speech or of gesture or in a memorable phase of the mind itself."[102] Since art is based on such unexpected revelations of character and situation, Stephen Dedalus deduces the role of every writer to be the recording of "these epiphanies with extreme care, seeing that they themselves are the most delicate and evanescent of moments."[103] Stephen then proceeds to emphasize the importance of these sudden manifestations. In the course of a mental journey to Aunt Sara's, his stream of consciousness assumes the form of an imaginary conversation with his uncle who reminds him of his old habit of registering epiphanies:

"Remember your epiphanies on green oval leaves, deeply deep, copies to be sent if you died to all the great libraries of the world, including Alexandria? Someone was to read them there after a few thousand years, a mahamanvantara. Pico della Mirandola like."[104]

Dr. Gogarty also narrates an incident in his autobiography when, in the course of an evening in a "snug" with Joyce, the latter begged to be excused and left the company. "I don't mind being reported", writes Gogarty, "but to be an unwilling contributor to one of his Epiphanies is irritating.

"Probably Father Darlington had taught him, as an aside in his Latin class—for Joyce knew no Greek—that 'Epiphany' meant 'a showing forth'. So he recorded under 'Epiphany' any showing forth of the mind by which he considered one gave oneself away."[105]

This concept of epiphany does not remain an abstract notion in the mind of Young Dedalus but assumes a concrete form when he tries to substantiate his theory with illustrations from his personal experiences. One misty evening, when he is walking through Eccles' Street, brooding over the attitude of women towards religion as being a mixture of cowardice and fear, he suddenly overhears a snatch of conversation between a young gentleman and a young woman.

"The Young Lady—(drawling discreetly) . . . O, Yes . . . I was . . . at the . . . cha . . . pel . . .

The Young Gentleman—(inaudibly) . . . I . . . (again inaudibly) . . . I

The Young Lady—(softly) . . . O . . . but you're . . . ve . . . ry . . . wick . . . ed . . ."[106]

On hearing these words, a sudden revelation of the essence of what he had been thinking for a long time, dawns within his consciousness. This moment of sudden "showing forth", he calls epiphany. The second instance cited by him is of the

Ballast Office Clock which, in a moment of epiphany, acquires new significance: glimpses at that clock will then appear to be "the gropings of a spiritual eye which seeks to adjust its vision to an exact focus."[107]

This theory of epiphany, it may further be seen, also seems to parallel Virginia Woolf's notion of reality as revealing itself in unexpected visionary flashes. In a central passage in *A Room of One's Own* she elaborates her theory of what may be called "evanescent reality":

"What is meant by 'reality'? It would seem to be something very erratic, very undependable—now to be found in a dusty road, now in a scrap of newspaper in the street, now a daffodil in the sun. It lights up a group in a room and stamps some casual saying . . . But whatever it touches, it fixes and makes permanent . . . Now the writer, as I think, has the chance to live more than other people in the presence of this reality. It is his business to find it and collect it and communicate it to the rest of us."[108]

And among the outstanding examples of this view of reality, she includes *A la recherche du temps perdu* which stresses the importance of intuition in creative writing. It is, therefore, easy to recognize a certain correspondence between Virginia Woolf's "evanescent reality", Proust's "intuition" and Bergson's *l'intuition philosophique*.

Joyce, therefore, by using a new term has unnecessarily introduced an element of ambiguity, for epiphany in many respects parallels intuition. In the *Portrait*, Stephen Dedalus drops this term altogether and uses its more familiar form—intuition. It is through an intuitional awareness that Stephen hopes some day to apprehend reality in a flash of aesthetic vision:

"He wanted to meet in the real world the unsubstantial image which his soul so constantly beheld. He did not know where to seek it or how, but a premonition which led him on told him that this image would, without any overt act of his, encounter him."[109] And in "that magic moment" he would

be completely transformed. That this intuitional moment
bears a certain resemblance to an epiphanic showing forth of
reality may be seen from another extract from the *Portrait*.
Stephen has been brooding over the "essence of beauty",
while his mind is wrapped in disquieting thoughts:

"His thinking was a dusk of doubt and selfmistrust, lit up
at moments by *the lightnings of intuition,* but lightnings of so
clear a splendour that in those moments the world perished
about his feet as if it had been fire-consumed; and thereafter
his tongue grew heavy and he met the eyes of others with
unanswering eyes, for he felt that the spirit of beauty had
folded him round . . ."[110]

These "lightnings of intuition" appear to represent
Stephen's earlier concept of epiphany, and in this sense
embrace every transcendental awareness of phenomena. Such
moments are obviously transitory[111] ("little daily miracles,
illuminations, matches struck unexpectedly in the dark",
reflects Lily Briscoe in *To the Lighthouse*[112]), and an artist
who could remain in a perpetual state of intuitive perception
would be such as the world has never yet seen.

These epiphanies or flashes of intuition hold up, as it were,
certain moments out of the flowing stream of experience for
a more intense contemplation. These are moments of unexpected spiritual awakening, moments which enable the
mind to transcend all reason and perceive phenomena in a new
perspective. They embody the same principle of literary
composition which, in Bergson's words, enables a novelist to
conceive a character "all at once, in its entirety",[113] and
present it "in its flowing through time".[114] Art, observes
Bergson, is itself the outcome of such sudden and direct
revelations of reality, implying a virginal "purity of perception" which reaches its culmination in moments of
epiphany.[115] Buried under the thick layer of "habit or
action", lie dormant such moments of sudden "showing
forth" over which reason has no control. "The slow progress

of mankind", says Bergson in *Laughter*, "in the direction of an increasingly peaceful social life has gradually consolidated this layer, just as the life of our planet itself has been one long effort to cover over with a cool and solid crust the fiery mass of seething metals. But volcanic eruptions occur."[116]

Of precisely such volcanic nature are "epiphanies" or intuitive "eruptions", which reveal to the novelist a vision of reality not otherwise apprehensible.

* * * * * *

In *Laocoon*, Lessing makes a distinction between painting and poetry as deriving from two distinctly different attitudes in art; whereas one is based on co-existence in *space*, the other is exclusively related to a realization of sequence in *time*. Each category of art, consequently, implies a different set of values, although an artist working in one medium may occasionally suggest, with a view to creating certain effects, values normally attributed to the other. This space-time polarity is as fundamental to any aesthetic theory as to any system of metaphysics, and in the work of James Joyce as in the entire thought of Bergson, space and time are presented as contraries, with durational flux as the only true reality. Whereas space is synonymous with matter, externality and convention, *la durée*, on the other hand, represents spirit, inner reality and free will. The stream of consciousness in fiction is a technique to render in a suitable medium this durational aspect of experience.

Although *Finnegans Wake* is not a stream of consciousness narrative, its treatment and presentation of flux makes it as significant as any of the earlier writings of James Joyce. This novel—if it can be called one at all—may be understood in terms of space-time polarity round which revolve all its episodes and characters. The concept of space-time, it may be mentioned here, implies the four dimensional continuum, binding into a unity three dimensional space to time which now becomes the fourth dimension. In accepting this post-Newtonian theory of relativity, Joyce seems to align himself with such thinkers as Einstein and Minkowski, according to whom nothing can be conceived of as physical apart from space-time. Joyce, however, like other stream of consciousness novelists, goes a step further in treating duration as the only determining factor in assessing human experience. He could have said, like Proust, that his aim as a novelist is to isolate time—"*that invisible substance.*"

Joyce's treatment of space-time polarity in *Finnegans Wake* shows his interest in the philosophic theories of Nicholas of Cusa (a fifteenth century philosopher-mystic) and Bruno of Nola (a sixteenth century philosopher) both of whom believed in the ultimate coincidence of all contraries. According to these Italian thinkers, reality emerges "by the coincidance of their contraries reamalgamerge in that indentity of undiscernibles . . ."[117] The contrapuntal nature of space and time is represented in a multitude of symbolic characters and episodes. For instance, as an introvert, indrawn, self-absorbed author Shem symbolizes duration, as against Shaun who is a space-oriented successful man of the world. Swift-Sterne, Caseous-Burrus, Stephen-Bloom, Dolph-Kev, Castor-Pollux, Guelf-Ghibelline, York-Lancaster, Cain-Abel, the "Gripes" and the "Mookse", the "Gracehoper" and the "Ondt", Glugg-Chuff, Jerry-Kevin, etc. are other polarized couples symbolizing time and space respectively. Again, in the scene where Yawn is held under inquest, the witness against him alludes to the World Tree which appears to be another symbol of *durée créatrice* ("that exquisitive creation and her leaves . . . sinsinsinning since the night of time and each and all of their branches meeting and shaking twisty hands all over again in their new world through the germination of its gemination . . ."[118]); whereas the vast monolith closeby symbolizes pace.[119]

This conflict between space and time is suggested towards

the end of "chapter" five when the Scotland Yard "inquiries pointed out ——→ that they ad bîn 'provoked' ay ∧ fork, of à grave Brofèsor; àth é's Brèak —— fast —— table[120]; acùtely profèssionally *piquéd*, to=introdùce a notion of time [ùpon à plane (?) sù' fàç'e'] by pùnct! ingh oles (sic) in iSpace?!"[121]

In a subsequent chapter the space-time conflict assumes still more significant proportions in the ironical references of Professor Jones, the spatialist, to his contemporary time-philosophers. Although his tirades are launched against both Bergson and Einstein, it is the former who emerges in the course of this controversy as his real counterpart, since it is not so much against the space-time continuum of Einstein that the Professor directs his vitriolic criticisms as against "Bitchson" who presents an exclusively durational attitude towards reality.

Professor Jones's scholarly defence of space forms the text of an evasive reply to a question asked by one of his pupils, "a poor acheseyeld from Ailing",[122] as to how he could save his soul. The reply turns out to be an erudite exposition of the "Dime-Cash problem" which may be divided into three parts: (a) a preliminary analysis of the general principles involved in the problem, (b) a fable called "The Mookse and the Gripes" and (c) the story of Burrus and Caseous. The preliminary phase of this learned discourse, however, states the basic controversy between the neo-classical spatialists and contemporary time-philosophers. Professor Jones opens the discussion with a direct reference to Bergson, whose theory of durational flux he has already refuted in an earlier treatise:

"But before proceeding to conclusively confute this begging question it would be far fitter for you, if you dare! to hasitate to consult with and consequentially attempt at my disposale of the same dime-cash problem elsewhere natural-istically of course, from the blinkpoint of so eminent a spatialist."[123] And then he proceeds to argue how the time-philosophy of Bergson is not without its spatial implications.

". . . you will here notice, Schott, upon my for the first remarking you that the sophology of Bitchson while driven as under by a purely dime-dime urge is not without his cashcash charackterricksticks . . ."[124] This is followed by another veiled allusion to Proust's *A la recherche du temps perdu* in a parenthesis ("who the lost time we had the pleasure we have had our little *recherché* brush with . . ."[125])

Furthermore, the time-philosophy of Bergson ("the romantic in rags"), according to Professor Jones, is fluid and ambiguous, seldom yielding any concrete or tangible results:

"What the romantic in rags pines after . . . is the poorest commonon-guardiant waste of time . . . I would like the neat drop that would malt in my mouth but I fail to see *when* . . . since his man's *when* is no otherman's *quandour* (Mine, dank you?) while, for aught I care for the contrary, the all is *where* in love as war . . ."[126]

In brief, Professor Jones (the Shaun type) belongs to the school of neo-classicists like Wyndham Lewis,[127] whereas "Bitchson" represents a time-oriented outlook on life.

And so ends one phase of this controversy between Professor Jones and Bergson, leading to the former's new version of the parable "The Mookse and the Gripes" with a suggestive beginning: "Eins within a space and a wearywide space it wast ere wohned a Mookse".[128] The central theme of this story again revolves round space-time polarity symbolized by the "Mookse" and the "Gripes".

"By the watch, what is the time, pace"? (ask the Gripes). To which the Mookse returns a provocative reply: "Quote awhore? That is quite about what I came on *my* missions with *my* intentions *laudibiliter* to settle with *you*, barbarousse. Let thor be orlog."[129]

So we again hear in this parable the voice of Professor Jones, and overtones from the earlier Cad-Assailant-Beggar theme. Professor Jones then concludes his eloquent lecture by protesting against the tendency of such misguided singers as Caseous (the Shem type) to subordinate space to time in their tragic lyrics:

"Of course the unskilled singer continues to pervert our wiser ears by subordinating the space-element, that is to sing, the *aria*, to the time-factor, which ought to be killed, *ill tempor*. I should advise any unborn singer who may still be among my heeders to forget her temporal diaphragm at home (the best thing that could happen to it!) and attack the roulade with a swift *colpo di glottide* to the lug . . . and then, O! on the third dead beat, O! to cluse her eyes and aiopen her oath and see what spice I may send her . . ."[130]

It may be easily seen how by making Professor Jones spatialize music, the purest of all temporal arts, Joyce clearly exposes his (Professor Jones's) entire thesis. Music, on the other hand, provides Bergson with some of his most suggestive analogies in representing experience as a process of symphonic cumulation which cannot be analysed in terms of "dead beats" or discrete simultaneities.

It is true that Joyce, like Sterne, makes great play with irony and parody, often adopting an ambivalent attitude towards his subject. The apparent comic tone and intention of the passages quoted above cannot be mistaken. But like Sterne in *Tristram Shandy* and Virginia Woolf in *Orlando*, he also implies a certain degree of seriousness in his parodic and ironical presentation of spatial and temporal habits of thought in *Finnegans Wake*. Joyce need not be too closely associated with Stephen Dedalus[131] or Shem, although, according to Harry Levin, "from Shem to Seumas to James is an easy modulation for Joyce".[132] Both Stephen Dedalus and Shem are, in a typical Bergsonian-Proustian sense, "giants immersed in time". Whereas Shaunian space only divides, measures and calculates, Shemian *durée* remains a process of eternal renewal. But in *Finnegans Wake* Joyce, whatever his bias, impersonally comes out for their ultimate union.

Interpreted in terms of Bergson's theories of *mémoire par excellence*, language and *la durée*, the work of James Joyce acquires a new perspective and meaning not otherwise discernible. Like Dorothy Richardson and Virginia Woolf, he belongs to "the Pure River Society"[133] (to borrow his own phrase), and his primary intention as a literary artist is to render in a new fluid medium "the constant of fluxion",[134] creating "always something new".[135] The predominant tense in the work of James Joyce, as of Gertrude Stein's, is always "the prolonged present". "Then's now with now's then in tense continuant."[136]

Joyce is perhaps the most distinguished exponent of *le roman fleuve*, though he was not consciously influenced by Bergson's theories. To speculate on his "borrowings" from the French philosopher would be straying into the bypaths of academic criticism. The important point to note is that his work, like that of Dorothy Richardson and Virginia Woolf, provides yet another example of parallelism between the Bergsonian flux and the stream of consciousness technique. In this chapter Bergsonism has been suggested as a useful clue to the mystery of "the steady monologuy of the interiors" and their "pardonable confusion",[137] and it is hoped that "by the light of philophosy . . . things will begin to clear up a bit one way or another . . ."[138]

* * * * * *

Notes

CHAPTER ONE

1. H. J. Muller, *Modern Fiction*, N.Y., 1937, p. 314.
2. Wladimir Weidlé, *The Dilemma of the Arts* (Translated by Martin Jarrett-Kerr), London, 1948, pp. 98-99.
3. Oswell Blakeston, 'Sang-Freud' or 'The Thought-Stream Novel', *The Bookman*, Vol. LXXXVII, No. 517, October 1934, p. 36. Another contemporary critic remarks, "Indeed we should not look for a clearer justification for the modern novel than in Jung's writing"; Melvin Friedman, 'Freud and Jung: the Problem of Consciousness', *Stream of Consciousness: a Study in Literary Method*, New Haven, 1955, p. 120.
4. Oswell Blakeston, *Ibid*, p. 36. Or it may be the reader who is the psychiatrist "to whom the unfortunate writer is telling everything he knows, in the hope that the welter will mean something to the listening specialist. The author is apparently the patient", Katherine F. Gerould, 'Stream of Consciousness', *Saturday Review of Literature*, Vol. 4, No. 13, N.Y., October 22, 1927, p. 233.
5. Pelham Edgar, 'The Stream of Consciousness', *The Art of the Novel*, N.Y., 1933, pp. 320-337.
6. F. J. Hoffman, *Freudianism and the Literary Mind*, Louisiana, 1945, pp. 127-129. See also, Edward Wagenknecht, 'Stream-of-Consciousness', *Cavalcade of the Novel*, N.Y., 1949, pp. 505-532, where he discusses Dorothy Richardson 'On the Stream', James Joyce 'Below the Stream', and Virginia Woolf 'The Stream and the World'.
7. Robert Humphrey, 'Stream of Consciousness—technique or genre', *Philological Quarterly*, Vol. XXX, October 1951, p. 437.

8. Robert Humphrey, *Stream of Consciousness in the Modern Novel*, Berkeley and Los Angeles, 1955, p. 21.

9. Lawrence E. Bowling, 'What is the stream of consciousness technique?' *Publications of the Modern Language Association*, Vol. LXV, No. 4, June 1950, p. 345.

10. J. W. Beach, 'Stream of Consciousness', *The Twentieth Century Novel*, N.Y., 1932, p. 517.

11. Obvious from a plethora of psycho-analytical terminology in the works of these novelists. See also, D. N. Morgan, 'Psychology and Art Today', *Journal of Aesthetics and Art Criticism*, Vol. 9, Dec., 1950, pp. 81-96.

12. Extract from J. M. Murry's review of *Ulysses* quoted by H. Gorman in *James Joyce*, London, 1949, p. 290.

13. J. W. Beach, *The Twentieth Century Novel*, p. 388.

14. Says Dr. Joseph Collins in his review of *Ulysses*: "I have learned more psychology and psychiatry from it than I did in ten years at the Neurological Institute", quoted in Herbert Gorman's *James Joyce*, London, 1949, p. 299.

15. Intuition, it may be remembered, has hardly any place in the Freudian system of thought.

16. See, for instance, A. A. Mendilow's *Time and the Novel*, London, 1952; particularly, Chapter 7 'The time-values of fiction'.

17. E. W. Hawkins, 'The Stream of Consciousness Novel', *The Atlantic Monthly*, Vol. 138, September 1926, pp. 356-360.

18. J. Isaacs, 'The Stream of Consciousness', *An Assessment of Twentieth-Century Literature*, London, 1951, p. 78.

19. *Ibid*, p. 87. Isaacs shows how Virginia Woolf's phrases "luminous halo", "semi-transparent envelope", are suggested in Stevenson's "soft iridescence of the luminous envelope" or "the aerial envelope".

20. Herbert Muller, 'Impressionism in Fiction', *The American Scholar*, Vol. 7, No. 3, Summer 1938, p. 357.

21. Translated by F. L. Pogson as *Time and Free Will*, London, 1910. Some critics of contemporary art have also attempted to relate the basic impulse of post-impressionism to Bergson's philosophy. See, for instance, Henri Seroúya's book *Initiation à la peinture d'aujourd'hui*, "Certains côtés de l'impressionnisme

. . . la façon de saisir l'impression spontanée, se rattachent au Bergsonisme", Paris, 1931, p. 70.

22. Edmund Wilson, *Axel's Castle*, N.Y., 1947, p. 205.

23. *Ibid*, p. 204.

24. It would be futile to establish the influence of Bergsonism on Symbolism or vice versa, both movements being almost simultaneous manifestations of the *Zeitgeist*. See also Edouard Dujardin, *Le Monologue Intérieur*, Paris, 1931, p. 95.

25. S. M. Eisenstein, 'An American Tragedy', *Close Up*, Vol. 10, No. 2, June 1933, pp. 120-121. Mr. Eisenstein observes how the *monologue intérieur* has exercised "a profound influence on the purely technical methods" (cinematic), and after referring to Joyce's new technique in *Ulysses*, cites an interview with him on its use in his production of 'An American Tragedy'.

26. Harry Levin, *James Joyce*, Connecticut, 1941, p. 88; also pp. 87-112. See a more detailed discussion of "Time- and Space-Montage" in terms of "multiple-view", "slow-ups", "fade-outs", "cutting", "close-ups", etc., in Robert Humphrey's *Stream of Consciousness in the Modern Novel*, Berkeley and Los Angeles, 1955, pp. 49ff.

27. Another popular exposition of the new technique is in terms of music. See Friedman, 'The Analogy with Music', *Stream of Consciousness: a Study in Literary Method*, New Haven, 1955, pp. 121-138. See also Vernon Hall, 'Joyce's Use of Da Ponte and Mozart's Don Giovanni', *PMLA*, Vol. 66, 1951, pp. 78-84.

28. Joseph Collins, *The Doctor Looks at Literature*, N.Y., 1923.

29. P. Lambert, 'L'éxile: Satire on current literary freaks', *Sewanee Review*, Vol. 40, October 1932, pp. 415-424.

30. Louis Hasley, 'The Stream of Consciousness Method', *Catholic World*, Vol. 146, November 1937, pp. 210-213.

31. "In *Les Lauriers sont coupés*, Joyce told me, the reader finds himself, from the very first line, posted within the mind of the protagonist, and it is the continuous unfolding of his thoughts which, replacing normal objective narration, depicts to us his acts and experiences. I advise you to read *Les Lauriers sont coupés*". Stuart Gilbert, *James Joyce's 'Ulysses'*, London, 1930, p. 24.

32. Edouard Dujardin, *Le Monologue Intérieur*, Paris, 1931, p. 33.

33. Victor Egger, *La Parole Intérieure*, Paris, 1904 (First published 1881'), pp. 1, 71, 113. For distinction between 'la parole intérieure' and 'la parole extérieure', see also G. Ballet, *Le Langage Intérieur*, Paris, 1886, p. 23.

34. Edouard Dujardin, *Le Monologue Intérieur*, p. 59.

35. *Ibid*, p. 68 (Italics mine).

36. *Letters of Proust* (Translated by Mina Curtiss), London, 1950, p. 188 (Italics mine).

37. Proust, *Time Regained* (Translated by Stephen Hudson), London, 1951, pp. 429, 430, 433.

38. André Gide, *The Coiners* (Translated by D. Bussy), London, 1950, p. 206.

39. Jules Romains, *The Death of a Nobody* (Translated by Desmond MacCarthy), London, 1914, p. 5.

40. Italo Svevo, *The Nice Old Man and Other Stories* (Translated by L. Collison-Morley), London, 1930, p. 153. It should be interesting to compare this with Bergson's statement in *Durée et Simultanéité* (Paris, 1922, p. 60): "Le mathématicien, il est vrai, n'aura pas à s'occuper d'elle, puisqu'il s'intéresse à la mesure des choses et non pas à leur nature. Mais s'il se demandait ce qu'il mesure, s'il fixait son attention sur le temps lui-même, nécessairement il se représenterait de la succession . . ."

41. Virginia Woolf, *Orlando*, London, 1949, p. 91.

42. Thomas Wolfe, *Look Homeward Angel*, N.Y., 1929.

43. Gertrude Stein, *Composition as Explanation*, London, 1926, p. 17.

44. Even the title of Thomas Wolfe's novel *Of Time and the River* (N.Y., 1935) suggests this new realization of experience as flux.

45. Italo Svevo, *The Nice Old Man* etc., London, 1930, p. 152.

46. Virginia Woolf, *The Waves*, London, 1950, p. 187.

47. Bergson, *Time and Free Will* (Translated by F. L. Pogson), London, 1950, p. 104 (First English translation 1910).

48. Bergson, *Matter and Memory* (Translated by N. M. Paul & W. S. Palmer), London, 1913, p. 178.

49. *Time and Free Will*, p. x.

50. Stanley Jones, *The Metaphysical Basis of the Work of Marcel Proust*, Unpublished Ph.D. Dissertation, 1949, Cambridge University Library.

51. *Letters of Proust*, pp. 203-204.

52. "My novel is not a work of ratiocination; its least elements have been supplied by my sensibility . . .", *Ibid*, p. 189.

53. Proust, *Swann's Way* (Translated by S. Moncrieff), Pt. 1, London, 1922, p. 57.

54. Proust, *The Guermantes Way* (Translated by S. Moncrieff), Pt. 1, London, 1925, pp. 117-118.

55. *Letters of Proust*, p. 332.

56. *Henri Bergson: essais et témoignages recueillis* (Ed. Béguin & Thévenaz), Neuchatel, 1943, p. 125.

57. Fernand Vial, 'Le Symbolisme Bergsonien du Temps dans l'oeuvre de Proust', *PMLA*, Vol. LV, December 1940, p. 1191.

58. *Letters of Proust*, p. 165.

59. It may here be noted that Proust himself was the first to use the term 'romans bergsoniens', which seems to be only another name for the stream of consciousness novel.

60. Quoted by Martin Turnell in his book *The Novel in France*, London, 1950, p. 189.

61. *Matter and Memory*, pp. 217-225.

62. T. E. Hulme, *Speculations*, London, 1924, p. 149 (Italics mine).

63. *Ibid*, p. 263.

64. Jules Romains, *The Death of a Nobody* (Translated by Desmond MacCarthy), London, 1914, p. VI.

65. Bergson, *Creative Evolution* (Translated by Arthur Mitchell), London, 1913, p. 188. It is not our intention here to suggest that James was in any sense influenced by Bergson or vice versa. These two "frères pensées", working independently arrived at similar conclusions. At a later stage they came to recognize in each other the same philosophic impulses. The extent to which William James later on came to corroborate Bergson's view of mobile reality may be seen from his marginal notes in the text of a copy of *L'Évolution Créatrice* which the latter presented "à M. le Prof. William James, son devoué admirateur—Henri Bergson". From the markings in ink and

pencil, one is surprised to observe how closely the curves and lines of their respective philosophies synchronize with each other. For instance, on p. 369 of this copy James underlines: "Le temps est invention ou il n'est rien du tout"—and adds on p. 100: "Vision is to the eye what movement is to a path". This copy of Bergson's *L'Évolution Créatrice* (Paris, 1907) is one of the James manuscripts in the Houghton Library, Harvard, Cambridge, Massachusetts.

66. May Sinclair, 'The Novels of Dorothy Richardson', *The Egoist*, Vol. 5, April 1918, p. 58.

67. William James, *The Principles of Psychology*, Vol. 1, London, 1907, p. 620 (First published 1890).

68. *Ibid*, p. 239.

69. *Ibid*, p. 281.

70. Virginia Woolf, 'Modern Fiction', *The Common Reader* (First Series), London, 1948, p. 189 (First published 1925).

71. *Ibid*, pp. 189-190.

72. *The Principles of Psychology*, Vol. 1, pp. 606-607.

73. William James, however, borrows this term from E. R. Clay's book *The Alternative* (London, 1882, p. 167) where he says, "The relation of experience to time has not been profoundly studied . . . The present to which the datum refers is really a part of the past—a recent past—delusively given as being a time that intervenes between the past and the future. Let it be named the specious present."

74. *The Principles of Psychology*, Vol. 1, p. 609.

75. Gertrude Stein, *Composition as Explanation*, London, 1926, pp. 16-17 (Italics mine). Cf. also with Bergson's definition of the "live present" in *Matter and Memory* (London, 1913), pp. 176-177.

CHAPTER TWO

1. Jacques Mercanton, 'Le Problème de L'Art', *Henri Bergson* (Ed. Béguin et Thévenaz), Neuchatel, 1943, p. 151.

2. Bergson, *Time and Free Will* (Translated by F. L. Pogson), London, 1950, p. 14 (First published in French 1889).

3. William James, *A Pluralistic Universe*, London, 1909, p. 227.

4. At the basis of all philosophical inquiry, says Bergson, is *l'émotion créatrice* which informs also his own entire thought "All philosophical work that is fruitful arises out of concentrated thought with pure emotion at its base," (At the banquet of the *Revue de Métaphysique et de Morale*, Dec., 27, 1923) quoted by Jacques Chevalier in *Henri Bergson* (Translated by L. A. Clare), London, 1928, p. 68.

5. Bergson, *La Pensée et le Mouvant*, Paris, 1934, p. 20. This particular essay 'Mouvement Rétrograde du Vrai' was first published in 1934, about 12 years after the publication of *A la recherche du temps perdu*.

6. Bergson, *An Introduction to Metaphysics* (Translated by T. E. Hulme), London, 1913, p. 6 (First published in French 1903).

7. *Ibid*, pp. 2-3.

8. *Ibid*, p. 59.

9. *Ibid*, p. 3.

10. *Letters of Proust* (Translated by Mina Curtiss), London, 1950, p. 313.

11. *An Introduction to Metaphysics*, p. 4.

12. Proust, *Time Regained* (Translated by Stephen Hudson), London, 1951, pp. 239-240 (First published in English 1931).

13. Bergson, *Laughter* (Translated by Brereton and Rothwell), London, 1911, p. 150.

14. These words are used here in a Bergsonian sense to imply the thick impervious layers of routine habits or actions that cover our innermost emotions.

15. *Laughter*, p. 152.

16. *Ibid*, p. 153.

17. *Ibid*, p. 156.

18. Virginia Woolf, *Mrs. Dalloway* (Phoenix ed.), London, 1950, pp. 33-34 (First published 1925) (Italics mine).

19. James Joyce, *Ulysses*, London, 1949, p. 742 (First published 1922).

20. *Laughter*, pp. 156-157.

21. *Ibid*, p. 157.

22. Virginia Woolf, *The Common Reader* (First Series), London, 1948, pp. 190-191.

23. *An Introduction to Metaphysics*, p. 8.

24. Bergson, *Mind-Energy* (Translated by Wildon Carr), London, 1920, p. 128.

25. Bergson, *Matter and Memory* (Translated by N. M. Paul & W. S. Palmer), London, 1913, p. 24 (First English translation 1911).

26. *Ibid*, p. 25.

27. *Ibid*, p. 194.

28. *Ibid*, p. 92.

29. *Letters of Proust*, p. 189.

30. *Matter and Memory*, p. 95.

31. *Matter and Memory*, p. 101.

32. Cf. Virginia Woolf's description of memory as "the seamstress, and a capricious one at that"; *Orlando*, London, 1949, p. 74.

33. Proust's claims to this distinction are scattered all over his work. Some of the key references are: *Swann's Way* (Translated by Scott Moncrieff), Pt. 1, London, 1922, p. 57; *The Sweet Cheat Gone* (Translated by Scott Moncrieff), London, 1930, p. 175; *Time Regained* (Translated by Stephen Hudson), London, 1931, pp. 213-215, 220, 275-7, 419.

34. See for instance, Justin O'Brien, 'La Mémoire Involontaire, Avant Marcel Proust', *Revue de Littérature Comparée*, Paris, 1939, pp. 19-36. Whereas he cites about nine instances from literature of the use of involuntary memory, he fails to refute Proust's claim against Bergson's. Instead, he reaffirms that the distinction between the two forms of memory does *not* appear in Bergson's philosophy.

35. *Letters of Proust*, p. 213 (Italics mine).

36. *Ibid*, p. 189.

37. *Ibid*, p. 189 (This letter is dated November? 1912).

38. Bergson, *Mind-Energy*, London, 1920, p. 94.

39. *Matter and Memory*, pp. 221-222.

40. *Ibid*, p. 219.

41. *Ibid*, p. 221.

42. Whereas Bergson admits association as one of the fundamentals of our psychic life, he rejects the thesis of the associationists that ideas can be treated as distinct and discrete elements capable of lending themselves to a convenient logical analysis. *Matter and Memory*, pp. 220 ff.

43. John Locke, *An Essay Concerning Human Understanding,* Vol. 1, Bk. 2, Chapter 'Of the Association of Ideas', Oxford, M.DCCC.XCIV, pp. 527-535. Sterne's indebtedness to Locke and his repeated emphasis on "duration" is treated in the chapter on Virginia Woolf.

44. Thomas Brown, *Lectures on the Philosophy of the Human Mind* (Lecture X), Edinburgh, 1820.

45. Bergson, *Time and Free Will,* pp. 132-133.

46. *Ibid,* p. 133.

47. *Ibid,* p. 133.

48. Bergson, *Creative Evolution* (Translated by Arthur Mitchell), London, 1913, p. 7.

49. "My mental state, as it advances on the road of time, is continually swelling with the duration which it accumulates: it goes on increasing—rolling upon itself, as a snowball on the snow", *Ibid,* p. 2.

50. Bergson, *Mind-Energy,* London, 1920, p. 44.

51. Bergson, *The Two Sources of Morality and Religion* (Translated by Ashley Audra and C. Brereton), N.Y., 1935, pp. 218-220.

52. *Ibid,* p. 242 (Italics mine).

53. Virginia Woolf, *The Waves,* London, 1950, p. 158.

54. *Ibid,* p. 55.

55. Virginia Woolf, *Mrs. Dalloway,* London, 1950, p. 59.

56. *Ibid,* p. 113.

57. *Ibid,* p. 193 (Italics mine).

58. Dorothy Richardson, *Pilgrimage,* Vol. 1, London, 1938, p. 68.

59. *Ibid,* p. 170.

60. James Joyce, *Ulysses,* London, 1949, p. 164.

61. Even Dorothy Richardson, like Joyce, occasionally coins a new word—"Rumbledumbledumble"—to render a sensation phonetically. *Pilgrimage,* Vol. 4, p. 503.

62. Bergson, *Creative Evolution,* p. 344.

63. Dorothy Richardson's protagonist, Miriam Henderson, is a keen critic of the novel. For her observations on the novelist's technique see *Pilgrimage,* Vol. 2, pp. 118, 130-131, etc.

64. "Idea that one could work out a theory of fiction . . .", *A Writer's Diary,* London, 1953, p. 216.

65. Shem, in many respects, is a prototype of Joyce, specially as

the author of his "usylessly unreadable Blue Book", James Joyce, *Finnegans Wake,* London, 1939, p. 179.

66. "J'ai demandé ensuite à Bergson s'il n'a pas l'intention de publier bientôt", writes Isaac Benrubi, "un ouvrage sur les problèmes de l'esthétique. Il me répondit: 'Ces problèmes m'intéressent à un haut degré, mais je suis trop vieux' . . .", *Henri Bergson* (ed. Béguin et Thévenaz), Neuchatel, 1943, p. 368.

CHAPTER THREE

1. Dorothy Richardson, 'Mr. Clive Bell's Proust', *The New Adelphi* (New Series), Vol. 2, No. 2, Dec-Feb, 1928-29, p. 161.
2. Letter to the author, dated August 10, 1952.
3. Dorothy Richardson, *Pilgrimage,* Vol. 1, London, 1938, p. 10.
4. George Santayana in his *Winds of Doctrine* (N.Y., 1913, p. 73) refers to Bergson's philosophy, rather derogatively, as mere "literary psychology", failing to realize, surprisingly enough as Santayana himself is a distinguished literary artist, that a philosophy need not lose its validity by seeking a less esoteric form of communication.
5. *Pilgrimage,* Vol. 1, London, 1938, pp. 10-11.
6. Goethe, *Wilhelm Meister,* Vol. 1, Pt. 2, Bk. 5, Chapter 7. This passage, her own translation from the original, is quoted by Dorothy Richardson as a suitable literary "manifesto" for the stream of consciousness novel. *Pilgrimage,* Vol. 1, p. 11 (Italics mine).
7. See also, Tancrède de Visan, 'La philosophie de M. Bergson et le lyrisme contemporain', *Vers et Prose,* Vol. XXI, 1910, pp. 125-40.
8. It may be noted that Dorothy Richardson is also a poet of some talent. Her poems have appeared in *Spectator, Life and Letters, Outlook, Fortnightly,* etc.
9. Dorothy Richardson, *Honeycomb,* London, 1917, pp. 125-27 (Italics mine).
10. Dorothy Richardson's keen interest in contemporary French

writers is also evident from the fact that she introduced to the English readers a translation of F. Ribadeau's *These Moderns* (London, 1932).

11. May Sinclair, 'The Novels of Dorothy Richardson', *The Egoist,* Vol. 5, April 1918, p. 58.

12. Title of a book by May Sinclair. She also published under the influence of Dorothy Richardson her novel, *Mary Olivier* (1919), which employs the stream of consciousness method of narrative.

13. May Sinclair, *A Defence of Idealism*, London, 1917, p. IX.

14. *Collected Stories of Katherine Mansfield*, London, 1948, pp. 524-525.

15. Dorothy Richardson, *The Tunnel*, London, 1919, pp. 157-158.

16. Critics (for instance, Harry Levin, *James Joyce*, Connecticut, 1941, Chapter 'Montage') have sometimes tried to trace the origin of the stream of consciousness technique to such early novelists as Fanny Burney, Samuel Richardson, Fielding, George Eliot and others, whereas in fact the device employed by these writers may be more appropriately termed mere 'memory digression'.

17. Richard Church, *An Estimate of Pilgrimage*, London, 1938, p. 7. J. C. Powys, however, claims exclusively for Dorothy Richardson's *Pilgrimage,* the title 'stream of consciousness novel', even withholding it from the work of James Joyce and Virginia Woolf. In a critical essay (*Dorothy Richardson,* London, 1931, p. 19) he remarks: "The search for 'originals' belongs rather to the 'antiquarianism' of literature than to the art of interpretation, but it is a fact worth noting . . . that while the academicians go on discussing 'the stream of consciousness' method, and using the work of Joyce and Proust, and even the work of Virginia Woolf, to illustrate it, it is not with Joyce, who strains it past breaking point, nor with Proust who, though his belief in it is implicit in the theory of literary art elaborated at the end of his last volume, never takes the risk of trusting it, and certainly not with Virginia Woolf that this method, which owes its very name to the work of Dorothy Richardson, is properly to be identified."

18. Bergson, *The Creative Mind* (Translated by M. L. Andison), N.Y., 1946, p. 152.
19. *Ibid*, p. 185.
20. Dorothy Richardson, 'Work in Progress', *Life and Letters*, Vol. 49, April 1946, pp. 20-44; 'Work in Progress', *Life and Letters*, Vol. 49, May 1946, pp. 99-114; 'Work in Progress', *Life and Letters*, Vol. 51, November 1946, pp. 79-88.
21. *The Creative Mind*, p. 177.
22. Dorothy Richardson, *Clear Horizon*, London, 1935, pp. 170-171.
23. Cf. Nietzche's statement: "'Being' is a fiction invented by those who suffer from becoming", *The Birth of Tragedy*, (Translated by W. A. Hausmann), London, 1909, p. XXVII.
24. *Clear Horizon*, pp. 171-172.
25. Dorothy Richardson, *Dimple Hill* (*Pilgrimage*, Vol. 4, London, 1938, p. 424). Italics mine.
26. Bergson, *An Introduction to Metaphysics*, p. 55.
27. Dorothy Richardson, *Dawn's Left Hand*, London, 1931, p. 166 (Italics mine).
28. Dorothy Richardson, 'Novels', *Life and Letters*, Vol. 56, March 1948, p. 189.
29. Dorothy Richardson, *Pilgrimage*, Vol. 1, p. 11.
30. Letter to this author dated August 10, 1952.
31. Dorothy Richardson, *Deadlock*, London, 1921, pp. 89-90 (Italics mine).
32. *Clear Horizon*, pp. 92-93 (Italics mine).
33. Dorothy Richardson, *The Tunnel*, London, 1919, p. 104.
34. Dorothy Richardson, *Interim*, London, 1919, p. 36.
35. *Deadlock*, p. 282.
36. Dorothy Richardson, *Backwater*, London, 1916, pp. 176-177.
37. If "silence, exile and cunning" are for Stephen Dedalus the prerequisites of creative composition, "silence" alone could define the tone and spirit of Dorothy Richardson's entire work. Her translation of Robert de Traz's book *Silent Hours* (London, 1934) is a further indication of her persistent emphasis on silence and contemplation.
38. *Backwater*, p. 206.
39. *Deadlock*, p. 66.

40. "All the letters are written while the hearts of the writers must be supposed to be wholly engaged in their subjects . . . so that they abound not only with critical situations, but with what may be called *instantaneous* descriptions and reflections", Samuel Richardson, *The History of Clarissa Harlowe*, Vol. 1, London, MDCCCLXXXIII, p. XI.
41. Samuel Richardson, *Sir Charles Grandison*, Vol. 1, London, MDCCCLXXXIII, pp. 143-144.
42. *The Tunnel*, pp. 185-188.
43. *Ibid*, p. 74.
44. Dorothy Richardson, *Honeycomb*, London, 1917, p. 153 (Italics mine).
45. *Ibid*, pp. 2-5.
46. Cf. "I was not traversing the same streets as those who were passing by; I was gliding through a sweet and melancholy past composed of so many different pasts . . .", Marcel Proust, *Time Regained*, p. 200.
47. *Clear Horizon*, p. 75 (Italics mine).
48. *Deadlock*, p. 176.
49. *An Introduction to Metaphysics*, p. 38.
50. *The Tunnel*, pp. 93-94.
51. *Clear Horizon*, p. 147 (Italics mine).
52. Bergson, *Matter and Memory*, pp. 176-177. Cf. Dorothy Richardson's statement: "The present can be judged by the part of the past it brings up", *Interim*. p. 200.
53. *Matter and Memory*, p. 212.
54. *Ibid*, p. 215.
55. *Ibid*, pp. 215-216.
56. *Clear Horizon*, p. 75.
57. *Ibid*, p. 75.
58. *Deadlock*, p. 49.
59. *Dawn's Left Hand*, p. 10.
60. Dorothy Richardson, *Revolving Lights*, London, 1923, p. 142.
61. *Interim*, p. 43.
62. *Clear Horizon*, p. 145.
63. *The Tunnel*, p. 265.
64. *Clear Horizon*, pp. 182-183.

65. L. A. Bisson, 'Proust, Bergson, and George Eliot', *Modern Languages Review*, Vol. XL, No. 2, April 1945, pp. 104-114.

66. H. B. Parkes, 'The Tendencies of Bergsonism', *Scrutiny*, Vol. 4, No. 4, March 1936, p. 424.

67. *Matter and Memory*, p. 70.

68. *Ibid*, p. 198.

69. *Ibid*, p. 94.

70. Bergson, *Laughter* (Translated by Brereton and Rothwell), London, 1911, pp. 151-154.

71. Bergson, 'Dreams', *Mind-Energy* (Translated by W. Carr), London, 1920, p. 92.

72. Endowed with a keen sensibility, Miriam resembles her creator in being a potential novelist and subtle critic. ("You've masses of material for Middles", Hypo tells her, "Criticism. You could do that on your head. Presently *novel*", *Pilgrimage*, Vol. 4, London, 1938, p. 239.

73. Dorothy Richardson, *Pointed Roofs*, London, 1915, p. 12.

74. *Backwater*, p. 143.

75. *The Tunnel*, p. 12.

76. *Pointed Roofs*, pp. 32-34.

77. *Backwater*, pp. 230-232.

78. *Matter and Memory*, p. 92.

79. *Backwater*, p. 232.

80. *Ibid*, p. 233.

81. *Clear Horizon*, pp. 182-183. (Italics mine).

82. Also cf. Joyce's analysis of *souvenir involontaire* in *Ulysses*, London, 1949, p. 403.

83. Virginia Woolf, *A Writer's Diary*, London, 1953, p. 69.

84. *Ibid*, p. 144.

85. *Ibid*, p. 139.

86. *Ibid*, p. 139. (Italics mine).

87. Also the title of a chapter in Virginia Woolf's study: *Roger Fry*, London, 1940.

88. *A Writer's Diary*, p. 69.

89. *Ibid*, p. 162.

90. *Ibid*, p. 210.

CHAPTER FOUR

1. To Winifred Holtby Virginia Woolf is supposed to have denied
    having read Bergson. Cited by W. Y. Tindall in *Forces in
    Modern British Literature*, N.Y., 1949, p. 305. Critics would,
    however, continue to argue: "Although Mrs. Woolf says that
    she has never read Bergson, it is clear that she could have been
    familiar with his ideas in the environment in which she lived,
    without recourse to his books", N. E. Monroe, *The Novel and
    Society*, North Carolina, 1941, p. 210.

2. Another critic is tempted by the marked Bergsonian character
    of Woolf's novels to assume Bergson's direct influence on her
    style etc. For instance, according to R. Gruber, her style in
    Mrs. Dalloway and *To the Lighthouse* is influenced by Bergson.
    "From the poetic rhythms of Browne and Lamb and De
    Quincey . . . she now assumes the Bergsonian rhythms . . .
    she is following carefully Bergson's definition of style . . .",
    Virginia Woolf, Leipzig, 1935, p. 50.

3. Floris Delattre, *Le Roman Psychologique de Virginia Woolf*,
    Paris, 1932, p. 137. In a footnote Delattre even goes to the
    extent of suggesting that many expressions from Mrs.
    Stephen's book *The Misuse of Mind* (London, 1922) later
    appear in the work of Virginia Woolf, particularly in *The
    Common Reader* (First Series, London, 1925). For instance,
    the statement, "This description (of what reality is) will be
    intelligible only if we are willing and able to make a profound
    change in our attitude" (from *The Misuse of Mind*, p. 12), is
    echoed in this sentence from *The Common Reader*, p. 299:
    "New books lure us to read them partly in the hope that they
    will reflect this re-arrangement of our attitude". There is
    obviously an element of exaggeration in this far-fetched
    comparison.

4. Floris Delattre, *Le Roman Psychologique* etc., pp. 136-137.

5. To what extent critics have been anxious to establish relation-
    ship between Bergson and Virginia Woolf may be seen from
    the following extract from an account by Pierre Stouls of
    Émile Blanche's interview with her: "Nous demandons

ensuite à J. E. Blanche quelle place la littérature française a tenue dans la formation de V. Woolf. On sait, en effet, qu'on a souvent prononcé le nom de Marcel Proust pour expliquer le caractère introspectif de son oeuvre, et celui de Bergson pour fonder sa théorie de l'inexistence de la conscience", Pierre Stouls, 'Entretien avec Jacques-Émile Blanche', *Impressions* (Hommage à Virginia Woolf), Paris, No. 19-20 January-February 1938, p. 20. The fact that she read Proust does not necessarily imply that she picked up rudiments of Bergson's theories in his work.

6. We have already observed how this book raised quite a stir in the literary circles of the day and was reviewed by Dorothy Richardson in *The New Adelphi*, Vol. 2, 1928-29, pp. 160-161.

7. Clive Bell, *Proust*, London, 1928, p. 54.

8. Eliot's *The Wasteland*, it may be recalled, was published in 1923 by Leonard and Virginia Woolf at the Hogarth Press.

9. In a letter to this author dated January 21, 1953, Eliot wrote: "I was certainly very much under his (Bergson's) influence during the year 1910-11, when I both attended his lectures and gave close study to the books he had then written". But how much, if anything at all, could Virginia Woolf have learned from Eliot about Bergson would still be uncertain and debatable.

10. Jules Romains, *The Death of a Nobody* (Translated by Desmond MacCarthy), London, 1914, p. iii.

11. *Ibid*, p. v.

12. See also Jean Blum, 'La philosophie de M. Bergson et la poésie symboliste', *Mercure de France*, Vol. 63, Sep. 15, 1906, pp. 201-207.

13. Edmund Wilson, *Axel's Castle*, N.Y., 1947, p. 21.

14. Bergson, *An Introduction to Metaphysics*, p. 59.

15. *Axel's Castle*, pp. 21-22.

16. In a letter to this author dated August 12, 1952.

17. In a letter to this author dated February 1, 1952.

18. Marcel Proust, *Time Regained* (Translated by Stephen Hudson), London, 1951, p. 433.

19. Henry James, 'London Notes', *Notes on Novelists*, London, 1914, p. 349.

20. Virginia Woolf, *The Common Reader* (Second Series), London, 1932, pp. 79-80. (Italics mine).

21. There are two views about Sterne's treatment of Locke's ideas in *Tristram Shandy*. According to Cross and Baird, the novel renders a serious presentation of the Lockean theory of duration and succession of ideas. "*Tristram Shandy* is Locke's *Essay Concerning Human Understanding* in a novelized form", says Theodore Baird, 'The Time-Scheme of *Tristram Shandy* and a Source', *Publications of the Modern Language Association*, Vol. LI, No. 3, Sep. 1936, p. 803. See also Cross, *The Life and Times of Laurence Sterne*, New Haven, 1925, p. 277.

    According to other commentators like D. W. Jefferson, "Sterne's attitude was . . . one of humorous interest", but he also adds "It is essential to the effect that the ideas and beliefs should have a basis of seriousness in the mind of the author . . .", '*Tristram Shandy* and the Tradition of Learned Wit', *Essays in Criticism*, Vol. 1, No. 3, July 1951, pp. 244, 243. It is, however, more plausible to believe that although Sterne wrote in a parodic style, he did subscribe to Locke's theories with a tangible degree of seriousness.

22. Laurence Sterne, *Tristram Shandy*, London, 1948, p. 151. (Italics mine).

23. Cf. William James's statement: "Such words as 'chain' or 'train' do not describe consciousness . . . It is nothing jointed; it flows", *The Principles of Psychology*, Vol. 1, p. 239.

24. Bergson, *Time and Free Will*, London, 1950, p. 100.

25. Virginia Woolf, *Mrs. Dalloway*, London (New Phoenix Ed.), 1950, pp. 54, 56.

26. Virginia Woolf, *The Voyage Out*, London, 1949, p. 144.

27. Virginia Woolf, *Night and Day*, London, 1950, p. 44.

28. These stories appeared under the title *Monday or Tuesday*, London, 1921.

29. Virginia Woolf, *Jacob's Room*, London, 1949, p. 131. (Italics mine).

30. *Ibid*, pp. 132-133. (Italics mine).

31. Bergson, *Matter and Memory*, p. 176.

32. *Jacob's Room*, p. 169. (Italics mine).

33. *Ibid*, p. 170.

34. *Ibid*, p. 171.
35. *Ibid*, p. 173. (Italics mine).
36. *Ibid*, p. 173. (Italics mine).
37. In view of its preoccupation with time, this novel was first entitled *The Hours*. V. Woolf, *A Writer's Diary*, London, 1953, p. 57.
38. Bergson, *Creative Evolution* (Translated by A. Mitchell), London, 1913, p. 23.
39. *Mrs. Dalloway*, p. 113.
40. V. Woolf, *To the Lighthouse*, London, 1949, p. 76. (First published 1927).
41. *Ibid*, p. 209.
42. Proust, *The Captive* (Translated by Scott-Moncrieff), Pt. 2, London, 1929, p. 249.
43. *To the Lighthouse*, pp. 318-320. (Italics mine).
44. *Ibid*, p. 229.
45. Unlike Dorothy Richardson, her interests in interweaving 'vision and design' are paramount. "The problem is how to bring Lily and Mr. R. together", she observes in her diary, "and make a combination of interest at the end", *A Writer's Diary*, p. 99. *La durée* is the principle which enables her to achieve this effect.
46. V. Woolf, *Orlando*, London, 1949, pp. 90-91. (Italics mine). (First published 1928).
47. *Ibid*, pp. 91-92.
48. *Ibid*, p. 92.
49. Marcel Proust, *Time Regained*, p. 238.
50. *Orlando*, p. 92.
51. *Orlando*, some commentators suggest, is a pure fantasy and its philosophical implications may not be taken seriously. "But the balance between truth and fantasy", observes V. Woolf, "must be careful", *A Writer's Diary*, p. 117. "*Orlando* est une fantaisie spirituelle", remarks J. J. Mayoux, "*Orlando* est . . . la peinture symbolique de la durée . . . en un sens est un 'Temps Retrouvé' . . .", *Revue Anglo-Américaine*, Vol. 7, No. 4, April 1930, p. 324.
52. *Orlando*, p. 243.
53. *Ibid*, p. 287. Cf. Sterne, "The ringing of the bell, struck like-

wise strongly upon the sensorium of my uncle Toby", *Tristram Shandy*, London, 1948, p. 93.

54. *Ibid*, p. 91. (Italics mine).
55. *Ibid*, pp. 274-275. (Italics mine).
56. *Ibid*, p. 277.
57. This word is here used in a Bergsonian sense to imply the eternal presence of all the past states of consciousness in the present moment of experience.
58. *Orlando*, pp. 291-294.
59. A. A. Mendilow, *Time and the Novel*, London, 1952, p. 231.
60. V. Woolf, *The Waves*, London, 1950, p. 169.
61. *Ibid*, p. 178.
62. William James, *The Principles of Psychology*, Vol. 1, p. 243.
63. *The Waves*, pp. 210-211.
64. *Ibid*, p. 194. (Italics mine).
65. V. Woolf, *The Years*, London, 1940, p. 43. (First published 1937).
66. *Ibid*, p. 241.
67. *Ibid*, p. 292.
68. *Ibid*, p. 396.
69. V. Woolf, *Between the Acts*, London, 1947, pp. 13-14. (First published 1941). Italics mine.
70. Marcel Proust, *Cities of the Plain*. (Translated by Scott-Moncrieff). Pt. 1, London, 1929, p. 152.
71. V. Woolf, *Mr. Bennett and Mrs. Brown*, London, 1924, p. 24.
72. V. Woolf, *The Haunted House*, London, 1943, p. 60.
73. *The Years*, p. 197.
74. *Ibid*, p. 232.
75. *Ibid*, p. 395.
76. *Between the Acts*, p. 14.
77. *Matter and Memory*, p. 72.
78. Marcel Proust, *Within a Budding Grove* (Translated by Scott-Moncrieff), Pt. 2, London, 1924, p. 264.
79. *Orlando*, pp. 73-74.
80. *Matter and Memory*, p. 102. (Italics mine).
81. *Orlando*, p. 74. (Italics mine).
82. *Ibid*, pp. 93-94. (Italics mine).

83. Note two vast movements of memory beginning each on pages 65 and 80 respectively: *Mrs. Dalloway*, London, 1950.

84. *Ibid*, pp. 55-56.

85. *Ibid*, p. 65.

86. *Ibid*, pp. 65-66.

87. *Ibid*, pp. 68-69.

88. *Ibid*, p. 71. (Italics mine).

89. *Matter and Memory*, p. 92.

90. V. Woolf, *To the Lighthouse*, pp. 265-67. (Italics mine). The "tunnelling process" seems to be her favourite device for evoking the past involuntarily, and she came by it, as she tells us in her diary, after long experimentation. "This is my prime discovery so far; and the fact that I've been so long finding it proves, I think, how false Percy Lubbock's doctrine is— that you can do this sort of thing *consciously*", *A Writer's Diary*, London, 1953, p. 61. (Italics mine).

91. Proust, *Time Regained*, p. 228.

92. Bergson, *Mind-Energy* (Translated by W. Carr), London, 1920, p. 56.

93. Virginia Woolf suggests this polarity through various symbols. Her novels are full of images such as a sword flashing, a hand raised high in the air, etc., symbolizing the moment arrested against fluid time or *la durée*. The lighthouse itself is a symbol of the static moment amidst ceaseless durational flux.

94. Bergson, 'L'intuition philosophique', *La Pensée et le Mouvant*, Paris, 1950, pp. 117-142.

95. *To the Lighthouse*, p. 164.

96. The novel as a form of literary composition performs, according to Bergson, the same function as intuition of counteracting the cramping influence of the intellect. "It must be noted", says Bergson, "that fiction, when it has the power to move us, resembles an incipient hallucination: it can thwart our judgment and reason, which are the strictly intellectual faculties", *The Two Sources of Morality and Religion* (Translated by R. A. Audra & C. Brereton), N.Y., 1935, p. 99.

97. *To the Lighthouse*, p. 24.

98. *The Voyage Out,* pp. 13-14.
99. *Mrs. Dalloway,* p. 194.
100. Bergson, *La Pensée et le Mouvant,* p. 138.
101. Bergson, *Creative Evolution* (Translated by A. Mitchell), London, 1913, p. 316.
102. Bergson, *La Perception du Changement,* Oxford, 1911, p. 25: "Nous nous représentons des notes juxtaposées à des notes sur une feuille de papier imaginaire".
103. *To the Lighthouse,* pp. 56-57. (Italics mine).
104. Mrs. Ramsay represents "the gifted, the inspired who, miraculously, lump all the letters together in one flash—the way of genius", the way of intuitive apprehension: *To the Lighthouse,* p. 58.
105. *Ibid,* p. 57.
106. *Ibid,* p. 15.
107. *Ibid,* p. 13.
108. *Ibid,* p. 46.
109. *Ibid,* p. 49.
110. *Ibid,* pp. 61-62.
111. *Ibid,* p. 82.
112. Bergson, *An Introduction to Metaphysics,* London, 1913, p. 6.
113. *To the Lighthouse,* p. 297.
114. *Ibid,* p. 83.
115. *Ibid,* p. 95.
116. *Creative Evolution,* p. 174.
117. *To the Lighthouse,* p. 279. (Italics mine).
118. *Mrs. Dalloway,* p. 11.
119. Proust, *Within a Budding Grove,* Pt. 1, p. 211.
120. *Time Regained,* p. 209.
121. *Ibid,* p. 214.
122. *Ibid,* p. 227.
123. V. Woolf, *The Common Reader* (1st. Series), London, 1948, p. 90.
124. Bergson, *Mind-Energy,* p. 45.
125. V. Woolf, *The Waves,* London, 1950, p. 183.
126. If a metaphysician were to realize personality in its ceaseless becoming, he would have to invent "fluid concepts"—"I mean supple, mobile and almost fluid representations always ready

to mould themselves on the fleeting forms of intuition", Bergson, *An Introduction to Metaphysics*, p. 18.

127. V. Woolf, *Orlando*, p. 277.

128. Maxime Chastaign, *La Philosophie de Virginia Woolf*, Paris, 1951, pp. 146-147.

129. Another commentator also presents the same fallacious point of view about Virginia Woolf to assert that she is essentially static and spatial in her philosophical outlook, and therefore anti-Bergsonian: J. W. Graham, 'A Negative Note on Bergson and Virginia Woolf', *Essays in Criticism*, Vol. VI, January 1956, pp. 70-74.

130. *Orlando*, p. 283. "It is the speed, the hot, molten effect", says Bernard, "the laval flow of sentence into sentence that I need", *The Waves*, p. 57.

131. *The Waves*, pp. 67-68. As originally conceived under the title *The Moths*, this novel was supposed to present "the idea of some continuous stream . . .", *A Writer's Diary*, p. 108.

132. *The Waves*, p. 81.

133. *Ibid*, p. 177. (Italics mine).

134. *Ibid*, p. 181. (Italics mine).

135. *To the Lighthouse*, p. 241.

136. *The Waves*, p. 187.

137. *Ibid*, p. 93.

138. *To the Lighthouse*, p. 246.

139. *Ibid*, p. 308.

140. *An Introduction to Metaphysics*, p. 9.

141. Bergson, *La Perception du Changement*, Oxford, 1911, p. 26.

142. V. Woolf, *The Common Reader* (1st. Series), London, 1925, p. 189.

CHAPTER FIVE

1. James Joyce, *Finnegans Wake*, London, 1939, p. 115: ". . . but we grisly old Sykos who have done our unsmiling bit on "alices, *when they were yung and easily freudened* . . ." (Italics mine). Also see, Pelham Edgar, 'Psycho-analysis and James Joyce', *The Art of the Novel*, N.Y., 1933, pp. 301-319; R. M.

Kain, 'The Stream of Life: Psychological Associationism', *Fabulous Voyager—James Joyce's Ulysses*, Chicago, 1947, pp. 131-141; and F. J. Hoffman's Freudian analysis of the work of James Joyce in 'Infroyce', *Freudianism and the Literary Mind*, Louisiana, 1945, pp. 114-148. According to M. J. Friedman, "*Finnegans Wake* is . . . the literary storehouse for Jung's theory", *Stream of Consciousness: a Study in Literary Method*, New Haven, 1955, p. 115.

2. "Professor Loewy-Brueller . . . in his talked off confession which recently met with such a leonine uproar", *Finnegans Wake*, p. 150.

3. "Solarsystemised, seriolcosmically", *Ibid*, p. 263.

4. Wyndham Lewis, *Time and Western Man*, London, 1927, p. 106.

5. In a letter to the author dated January 20, 1953, Mr. Stuart Gilbert, who knew Joyce very intimately, corroborates his acquaintance with Bergson's philosophical theories.

6. *Finnegans Wake*, p. 149.

7. James Joyce, *Exiles*, New York, 1951, p. 125.

8. Gertrude Stein, *Composition as Explanation*, London, 1926, p. 30. (Italics mine).

9. *Ibid*, p. 16.

10. *Finnegans Wake*, p. 186.

11. William James, *The Principles of Psychology*, Vol. 1, p. 609.

12. Bergson, *Matter and Memory*, pp. 176-177.

13. ". . . from the day when my brother left Dublin until the Great War sent him to Zurich, Svevo was the only man of letters with whom he was on terms of some intimacy", Stanislaus Joyce in his introduction to Svevo's novel, *As a Man Grows Older* (Translated by B. Zoete), London, 1932, p. XIII. And writes Renato Poggioli, "If there is a writer for whom the resurrected William James formula ('stream of consciousness'), and its French and literary equivalent, coined by Valéry Larbaud (*monologue intérieur*), are particularly apt, that writer is Italo Svevo": Poggioli's introduction to Italo Svevo's novel, *Confessions of Zeno* (Translated by B. Zoete), London, 1948, p. 4.

14. See Gilbert Highet, 'The Symbolist Poets and James Joyce', *The Classical Tradition*, Oxford, 1951, pp. 501-519.

15. Daniel-Rops, 'Une Technique Nouvelle: Le Monologue Intérieur', *Le Correspondant*, Paris, 1932, pp. 287-288.

16. Edmund Wilson, *Axel's Castle*, New York, 1947, p. 157.

17. *Ibid*, pp. 221-222.

18. *Letters of James Joyce* (Edited by Stuart Gilbert), London, 1957.

19. James Joyce, *A Portrait of the Artist as a Young Man*, London, 1950, p. 111. (First published 1916).

20. James Joyce, *Ulysses*, London, 1949, p. 46.

21. *Ibid*, p. 632.

22. C. G. Jung also testifies to the non-repetitive character of *Ulysses*: "As far as my glance reaches there are in those seven hundred and thirty five pages no obvious repetitions . . . the uninterrupted stream rolls by, and its velocity or precipitation grows in the last forty pages till it sweeps away even the marks of punctuation", *Ulysses—a monologue* (Translated by W. S. Dell), N.Y., 1949, pp. 1-2.

23. *Ulysses*, p. 79.

24. *Ibid*, p. 142. (Italics mine).

25. These three fragments Nos. XLI, XLII, LXXXI are from *The Fragments of the work of Heraclitus of Ephesus on Nature* (Translated from the Greek text of Bywater by G. T. W. Patrick), Baltimore, 1889, pp. 94, 104.

26. *Ulysses*, p. 394.

27. *Ibid*, p. 394.

28. *Ibid*, p. 396.

29. *Ibid*, p. 396.

30. Louis Gillet, 'Mr. James Joyce and his New Novel', *Transition*, No. 21, March 1932, p. 270. Describing a trip to the beach with Joyce, Lucie Noël says, "he was most relaxed when he was near the sea or a river", *James Joyce and Paul L. Léon: the story of a friendship*, N.Y., 1950, p. 30. "Joyce's feelings for all bodies of water amounted almost to nostalgia . . . Whenever he went on a holiday, he immediately looked for a river, a stream, or even a brook", Paul Léon, 'In memory of Joyce', *A James Joyce Yearbook*, Paris, 1949, p. 121.

31. In the course of a conversation with Max Eastman, Joyce told him that "into the prose of the little book in question—*Anna*

Livia Plurabelle—he had woven the names of five hundred rivers. The book in a certain sense is, or is about, a river", Max Eastman, *The Literary Mind*, N.Y., 1931, pp. 98-99.

32. Harry Levin, *James Joyce*, Connecticut, 1941, p. 194.

33. Edouard Dujardin, *Le Monologue Intérieur*, Paris, 1931, p. 47.

34. Bergson, *Creative Evolution*, pp. 322-323.

35. *Le Monologue Intérieur*, p. 68.

36. Bergson, *Mind-Energy* (Translated by W. Carr), London, 1920, p. 56. (Italics mine).

37. *Ulysses*, p. 716.

38. *Mind-Energy*, p. 45. (Italics mine).

39. *Finnegans Wake*, p. 159.

40. *Ibid*, p. 626.

41. *An Introduction to Metaphysics*, p. 9.

42. *Ibid*, p. 18.

43. *Finnegans Wake*, p. 107.

44. *Ibid*, p. 118. (Italics mine).

45. *Ibid*, p. 297.

46. *Ibid*, p. 103.

47. Title of a sub-section in *Transition* (No. 21, March 1932, pp. 284-325) devoted exclusively to the linguistic experiments of Joyce and others.

48. *Ibid*, p. 284.

49. *Ibid*, p. 298.

50. *Finnegans Wake*, p. 120.

51. *Creative Evolution*, p. 344.

52. Bergson, *Time and Free Will*, p. 130.

53. *Ibid*, p. 131. See also E. Le Roy, 'Critique of Language', *A New Philosophy : Henri Bergson*, London, 1913, pp. 167-184.

54. *Time and Free Will*, p. 133.

55. Bergson, *The Two Sources of Morality and Religion* (Translated by R. A. Audra & C. Brereton), N.Y., 1935, p. 242. (Italics mine).

56. *Ibid*, p. 38.

57. James Joyce, *Stephen Hero*, London, 1950, p. 23. It is true that Stephen, the potential artist in words, is portrayed by Joyce as especially sensitive to language and that it would be improper to equate Stephen's attitude with that of his creator

in maturity. Nevertheless, Stephen does speak for the artist on matters of this kind and it seems here that in depicting Stephen's reactions to words Joyce is expressing something of his own view of the artist's relation to his medium. One does not need to believe that Stephen is Joyce—an untenable belief, surely, though once popular—to see the significance of Stephen's attitude towards words, and art in general.

58. *Ulysses,* p. 606.
59. *Finnegans Wake,* pp. 628, 3.
60. Wyndham Lewis, *Time and Western Man,* London, 1927, p. 109.
61. *A Portrait of the Artist,* etc., p. 286.
62. *Ulysses,* p. 650.
63. *Ibid,* p. 183.
64. *Ibid,* p. 361.
65. *A Portrait of the Artist* etc., p. 88. (Italics mine).
66. *Ulysses,* p. 144.
67. *Ibid,* p. 244.
68. *Ibid,* p. 363.
69. Bergson, *Matter and Memory,* p. 92.
70. *Ulysses,* p. 145.
71. *A Portrait of the Artist* etc., p. 102. (Italics mine).
72. Although the first part of this passage is concerned primarily with "evil memories" it also represents adequately Joyce's general theory of memory.
73. *Ulysses,* p. 403. (Italics mine).
74. Also Cf. Dorothy Richardson's treatment of memory in *Pilgrimage,* Vol. 4, London, 1938, p. 368.
75. Bergson, *Creative Evolution,* p. 20.
76. *Ulysses,* p. 178. (Italics mine).
77. Wyndham Lewis, *Time and Western Man,* London, 1927, p. 132.
78. James Joyce, *Stephen Hero* (Ed. Theodore Spencer), London, 1950, p. 64. (First published July 1944).
79. *A Portrait of the Artist* etc., p. 200.
80. *Ibid,* p. 241.
81. *Ibid,* p. 242.
82. It may here be interesting to compare these three "phases of artistic apprehension" with Spinoza's three levels of know-

ledge: *Imaginatio, Ratio* and *Scientia Intuitiva*. *Claritas, l'intuition philosophique* and *Scientia Intuitiva* appear to belong to the same category.

83. Bergson's 'scheme' and 'image' seem to be synonymous respectively with Stephen's 'wholeness' and 'parts'.

84. Bergson, *Mind-Energy*, p. 173.

85. *Ibid*, pp. 173-174. (Italics mine).

86. *A Portrait of the Artist* etc., p. 242.

87. Bergson, *The Creative Mind* (Translated by M. L. Andison), N.Y., 1946, p. 273.

88. *A Portrait of the Artist* etc., pp. 242-243.

89. It may here be noted that Stephen's conception of art as *progressing* through three different forms is described only in the *Portrait;* in *Stephen Hero,* these forms are presented only as "three distinct natural kinds", p. 64.

90. *Portrait,* p. 244. (Italics mine).

91. *Ibid*, p. 244.

92. *Ibid*, p. 244. (Italics mine).

93. *Ibid*, p, 245.

94. *Ibid*, p. 193.

95. *Ibid*, p. 195.

96. *Ibid*, p. 244.

97. Stuart Gilbert, 'Art and Intuition', *Transition,* No. 21, March 1932, p. 217. Dr. Carr, in this article, is referred to as the translator of Benedetto Croce's *Logica.* He is also, it may be mentioned here, one of the most distinguished exponents of Bergson's thought.

98. In the *Portrait* this theory of "Esthetic" is expounded to Lynch, in *Stephen Hero* to Cranly.

99. *Stephen Hero,* p. 190.

100. "Car si l'intuition nous conduit à l'intérieure de la vie . . . et coïncider avec l'élan vital . . .", Albert Thibaudet, *Le Bergsonisme,* Paris, 1923, p. 57.

101. Bergson, 'L'Intuition Philosophique', *La Pensée et le Mouvant,* Paris, 1934, pp. 118, 119.

102. *Stephen Hero,* p. 188. (Italics mine).

103. *Ibid*, p. 188.

104. *Ulysses,* p. 37.

105. Oliver Gogarty, *As I was Going down Sackville Street,* Chapter XXII, London, 1937, p. 285.

106. *Stephen Hero,* p. 188.

107. *Ibid,* p. 188. Such a sudden revelation was experienced by Marcel Proust when he dipped a bit of madeleine into a cup of tea. "What is Joycean 'epiphany', after all", observes another critic, "but the equivalent of a Crocean 'moment of expression'? You see a clock daily; but at last you 'intuit' it. So Joyce . . .", Geddes MacGregor, 'Artistic Theory in James Joyce', *Life and Letters,* Vol. 54, 1947, p. 21.

108. Virginia Woolf, *A Room of One's Own,* London, 1929, pp. 165-166.

109. *A Portrait of the Artist* etc., p. 73.

110. *Ibid,* pp. 200-201.

111. The transitoriness of "the lightnings of intuition" is also referred to by Bergson in *Creative Evolution:* "These fleeting intuitions, which light up their object only at distant intervals . . . It is a lamp . . . which only glimmers now and then, for a few moments at most", p. 282.

112. V. Woolf, *To the Lighthouse,* p. 249.

113. *An Introduction to Metaphysics,* p. 3.

114. *Ibid,* p. 8.

115. Bergson, *Laughter* (Translated by Brereton & Rothwell), London, 1911, p. 159.

116. *Ibid,* p. 159.

117. *Finnegans Wake,* pp. 49-50.

118. *Ibid,* p. 505.

119. The tree and the stone, representing time and space respectively, seem to form ever-recurring symbols in *Finnegans Wake,* confronting the reader in a thousand disguised forms and indirect allusions. To mention only a few on pages: 103, 106-107, 113, 136, 146, 153, 159, 213, 216, 221, 259, 279.

Direct allusions to space-time polarity are equally numerous: ". . . wearing for the space of the time being some definite articles of evolutionary clothing . . .", *Finnegans Wake,* p. 109; "plenxty off time on his gouty hands and vacants of space at his sleepish feet", *Ibid,* p. 143; "A space. Who are you? The cat's mother. A time", p. 223; "from space to space, time after time", *Ibid,* p. 254; pp. 416-417; pp. 425, 462, 546, 558, 583, 599, and

> *"Your genus its worldwide, your spacest sublime!*
> *But, Holy Saltmartin, why can't you beat time?"* p. 419.

120. James Joyce here makes a veiled reference to Sherlock Holmes, and Oliver Wendell Holmes' series: *The Autocrat of the Breakfast Table,* London, 1865.

121. *Finnegans Wake,* p. 124.

122. *Ibid,* p. 148.

123. *Finnegans Wake,* p. 149.

124. In 'exposing' Bergson's time-philosophy as not being entirely free from spatial concepts, Jones seems to repeat the arguments of many critics of *la durée.* It is, for instance, argued that in spite of his repeated denunciation of intellect, Bergson himself does not infrequently borrow instruments of logic in establishing his theories.

125. *Finnegans Wake,* p. 149.

126. *Ibid,* p. 151.

127. Wyndham Lewis's book *Time and Western Man* is here parodied as *Spice and Westend Woman, Finnegans Wake,* p. 292.

128. *Ibid,* p. 152.

129. *Ibid,* p. 154.

130. *Ibid,* pp. 164-165.

131. Hugh Kenner has attempted to dissociate Joyce from the Dedalus-figure: 'Joyce's *Ulysses:* Homer and Hamlet', *Essays in Criticism,* Vol. II, No. 1, January 1952, pp. 85-104.

132. Harry Levin, *James Joyce,* Connecticut, 1941, p. 161. And he adds that "there can be no doubt that the autobiographical interest of the book is centred upon this character . . .", pp. 161-162. It may here be interesting to investigate into Shem's identity with James Joyce. Like his creator, he is a "tanner vuice" (*Finnegans Wake,* p. 182), "all ears" (p. 169), weak-sighted, "self exiled in upon his ego" (p. 184)—"Exexex! COMMUNICATED" (p. 172), producing from "his unheavenly body a no uncertain quantity of obscene matter not protected by copriright in the United Stars of Ourania" (p. 185) and writing "inartistic portraits of himself" (p. 182).

"Barnacled up to the eyes when he repented after seven,"

(*Finnegans Wake*, p. 423; J. Campbell and H. M. Robinson add in a footnote "Mrs. James Joyce, née Barnacle. This paragraph is a parody of Joyce's life", *A Skeleton Key to 'Finnegans Wake'*, London, 1947, p. 220), determined like Stephen Dedalus that he "will neither serve nor let serve, pray nor let pray" (*Ibid*, p. 188), "capped out of beurlads scoel" (p. 467), an allusion to Joyce's dismissal from Berlitz School), Shem appears to be only an impersonation of his creator.

"Immi ammi Semmi" (*Ibid*, p. 258), he declares and reiterates, "My shemblable! My freer!", suggesting clearly that it is through Shem and his durational character that Joyce appears to experience self-realization.

133. *Finnegans Wake*, p. 173.
134. *Ibid*, p. 297.
135. *Ibid*, p. 472.
136. *Ibid*, p. 598.
137. *Ibid*, p. 119.
138. *Ibid*, p. 119.

Index

Index